Looking God

Pursing Christ-Likeness

*God's original intent for Adam...
Our only goal today!*

By Daniel Isaiah Shalach

Unless otherwise indicated, all scripture quotations are taken from the King James Version of the Bible.

Scripture quotations marked (AMP) taken from the Amplified Bible, Copyright © 1954, 1958, 1962, 1964, 1965, 1987 by The Lockman Foundation. Used by permission. (www.Lockman.org)

Scripture quotations marked (MSG) are taken from *The Message*. Copyright © 1993, 1994, 1995, 1996, 2000, 2001, 2002. Used by permission of NavPress Publishing Group. All rights reserved.

Scripture quotations marked (NASB) are taken from the NEW AMERICAN STANDARD BIBLE®, Copyright © 1960,1962,1963,1968,1971,1972,1973,1975,1977,1995 by The Lockman Foundation. Used by permission.

Scripture quotations marked (NIV) are taken from THE HOLY BIBLE, NEW INTERNATIONAL VERSION®, NIV® Copyright © 1973, 1978, 1984, 2011 by Biblica, Inc.® Used by permission. All rights reserved worldwide.

Scripture quotations marked (NLT) are taken from the Holy Bible, New Living Translation, copyright © 1996, 2004, 2007 by Tyndale House Foundation. Used by permission of Tyndale House Publishers, Inc., Carol Stream, Illinois 60188. All rights reserved.

Scripture quotations marked (TLB) are taken from The Living Bible copyright © 1971. Used by permission of Tyndale House Publishers, Inc., Carol Stream, Illinois 60188. All rights reserved.

Scripture quotations marked (YLT) are taken from the Young's Literal Translation Bible, 1898.

The author has emphasized some words in Scripture quotations using italicized and or bold type.

Collins English Dictionary - Complete & Unabridged 10th Edition. Retrieved August 09, 2013, from Dictionary.com website:
http://dictionary.reference.com/browse/anxious
http://dictionary.reference.com/browse/retarded
http://dictionary.reference.com/browse/know

Strong's Exhaustive Concordance, James Strong. Published: 1890. Public Domain.

Strong's Hebrew and Greek Dictionaries, James Strong, (1822-1894). Permission to Quote: Electronic Edition STEP Files Copyright © 1998, Parsons Technology, Inc., all rights reserved.

Cover Design: Greg Kincaid, GK Grafx, www.Grafx.com

Body, Soul, Spirit graphic, courtesy of Minister Dale Fletcher, Faith and Health Connection

ISBN 978-0-9898638-0-3

Copyright © 2013, All rights reserved. Zoë Hope Training Center

www.LookingGod.com

Author's Note

I personally enjoy studying words in Greek and Hebrew as I read the Bible. I have found that some translations expound on the richness and depth of both languages at a greater degree than others. I enjoy the Amplified Bible for this reason.

Multiple translations of various Bible verses are presented throughout this book in order to provide a broader spectrum of the richness of the scriptures being referenced. I pray that you may grasp, apply and be transformed by new revelations that unfold.

I do want to say the best translator I have enjoyed using is Holy Spirit. He gives me insight that more often than not, is missed by many. Who better to guide me than the Author?

"The entrance *and* unfolding of Your words give light; their unfolding gives understanding (discernment and comprehension) to the simple" (Psalm 119:130 AMP).

Foreword

I believe that this book comes at a "divinely-appointed-time." There have been far too many Christian generations brought up with "poor-teaching" that has kept believers infantile, retarded, dwarfed-minded and immature in spirit. Many well-meaning preachers, leaders and pastors, have had an idea of what they wanted to express, yet they were unable to get it out because their "un-renewed mind" had dominance over their spirit. Due to fear, pride, "political correctness" or a host of reasons, others have decided to keep silent regarding this subject. In their inability to speak, God has allowed Daniel Isaiah to come out shouting from the roof tops declaring what God has wanted to say for the longest of days: "Looking God is what we should all desire!"

Why are "Christians" being defeated in the same areas that the world is? Why are believers who are called to be "more than conquerors" living a defeated life due to their own lustful desires? Why is the Body of Christ, who have been honored with the privilege of re-presenting heaven on earth as royalty and ambassadors, living as spiritual, mental and physical beggars, paupers and peasants?

The only reason believers are failing in our daily walk is due to a lack of knowing and embracing "our True identity" that gives and ignites True purpose. Every human heart asks the same questions: "Who am I?" "Why am I here?" and "Where am I going?" These are all questions regarding purpose, significance and meaning. For born-again believers, the "Good-News" is that this book will walk you step-by step through the answers to those questions that you've been asking. If you learn whose you are, then you'll learn who you are and why you are you.

When Daniel Isaiah honored me with the task of writing this forward, I of course humbly accepted. Daniel sent a rough-draft of this book by email for my review before the final print. He then left me an emphatic voicemail that made me smile, he said; "Brother I emailed you a copy of the book, but this is for your eyes only!" Well I can now say that I am exuberantly excited that this book is NO longer "just for my eyes only," but is now available for the whole wide-world to read!

Into and through these pages, Holy Spirit has interwoven from Daniel Isaiah's "renewed-mind," wisdom and kingdom principles that will set-you free, not only from your past, but the generational consequences that have been attached to it. The sound Biblical foundation that is being laid here is not only indispensable, but life-altering for any believer or non-believer; no matter how long you've walked with Christ or not yet walked with Him at all.

The Church body in general has been impotent for too long; their "works orientated" lifestyle has kept them on a spiritual milk diet. Daniel Isaiah serves a banquet feast of hearty "steaks and potatoes" for those who have "ears to hear" and are tired of just "growing-old" but are now ready to "grow-up!" Buckle-up in your seat belt and enjoy the exhilarating ride of renewing the mind as Holy Spirit wreaks havoc on your "old wine-skin" thought patterns and pours in His "new wine" into a "new wine skin," the renewed mind. "LOOKING GOD" will definitely look GOOD ON YOU!

Consumed,
Tito Santiago
Global Noize Ministries

Dedication

I dedicate this book to my Father who foreknew me and predestined me to grow into the likeness of Christ. To my Lord and Savior, Jesus the Christ, for resisting darkness, freeing me from the prison I was in, dying for me and then rising again so I can be empowered in my expectancy, and in that empowerment, I can represent Christ to all those I meet. To Holy Spirit for being that sweet still voice of wisdom, that loving Comforter and my Faithful Guide.

This book is also dedicated to my spiritual mother, Deborah Esther, who outside of Christ Himself, has proven to "love me the most." To David Jonathan and Hephzibah Joy who have prayed for me and added both to my growth and to His joy in me; you both have acted unselfishly with me and with no deceit. I love you both. My spiritual mentor and an example of focus, Leonard Williams, you have taught me the value of "staying thirsty." Thank you for your many prayers and constant unselfish outpouring and examples of what a Christ-like walk resembles.

To Cliff, "Call me Bob," Wolken for being the best younger brother a guy can have. You are taking a stand for Christ, which is well noted, and your love in Him is beyond words. To Derick, "I'm that dude" Kuilan, thank you for your obedience and love in the ministry and your undying support and faithfulness, may you never tap out. To Travis "Doc Jones" Gluckler, the Lord is not done with you yet, and you have a huge part to play in this "earth-suit" revolution; continue to "Stand Still." To Tito Santiago, thanks for listening and speaking when told to, I am sharper for having known you.

And to Samantha Lissette, the Son sets and rises in your eyes, and it is in this battle that God has chosen to have me formed. You are my true daughter and can never be forgotten. My Love for you, Samantha, grows deeper each day, the plans God has for you humble me.

ALL I want to be, and all I want to BE, are in Him.

Daniel Isaiah Shalach

Acknowledgements

I would like to acknowledge the work of the Holy Spirit in my life, and for this revelation I am working out as I write of His Almighty Majesty, Grace and Love.

I also would like to acknowledge Greg Kincaid from GK Grafx, www.GkGrafx.com, for his amazing art work.

Special acknowledgement to Gloria for her support and encouragement.

Introduction

Thank you for purchasing this book. My prayer is that you can read what I am sharing and go back to your prayer closet and ask Holy Spirit to make this real in your life as He gives you deeper revelation and His understanding. Then I hope you walk it out.

I came to the truths in this book many years ago. Then I was wrapped up with distractions that kept me away from walking these things out and making them real. About five years ago my Father was gracious enough to allow me to have my veil pulled back as I came into a revelation of who I was in Him and what I was actually born-again for.

It took me two years to submit to Him and to my spiritual covering. Truthfully, there are still many areas of my life I know He is working on, and more submission is needed on my part. The Truths in this book are things that I have walked out through experience. There are other Truths He has revealed to me, but I am still walking these out.

I am not trying to teach, but share, yet I know that, in sharing, I may also be teaching. I will accept either description of what I am doing as factual because I will never pass up an opportunity to sharpen another believer.

I recommend one thing, and one thing only with this book; that you pray and seek the Lord as you focus on Him. The things of this book are about Christ and how I am pressing in to become more like Him. This, however, takes revelation because Christ can never be taught; He can ONLY be revealed.

ALL I want to be, and all I want to BE, is in Him.

Daniel Isaiah

Table of Contents

Author's Note	iii
Foreword	iv
Dedication	vi
Acknowledgements	vii
Introduction	viii
Table of Contents	ix
Part One	2
Understanding I am not my own…	
Chapter 1	4
Wait…created in *whose* image?	
Chapter 2	9
What is man? Understanding how we were Created	
Chapter 3	19
Not sold out, but being "souled" out…	
Chapter 4	25
The bending of my ME…	
Part Two	31
Coming into an understanding	
Chapter 5	32
D.N.A vs. G.N.A	
Chapter 6	40
Growing in Him	
Chapter 7	52
Not all things are created equal	

Chapter 8 — 60
   Ministry vs. Majesty

Chapter 9 — 77
   Getting out of the way

Part Three — 81
   The end of the story and the beginning of a revolution

A Note from the Author — 83

Part One

Understanding I am not my own...

It was August of 2008. I was driving up US 1. It was around 8 PM. Not that late as far as late goes, but after a long day of ministry I was feeling the attraction of a hot shower and the calling of my bed. I was spent. I had a date with my pillow, and I was not going to cancel, or so I thought.

I was praying and speaking to the Lord when I first heard it. It was that same voice I had come to know as Holy Spirit. The same voice that had guided me so many times before. It whispered, "Go to the book store." I knew it was Holy Spirit, but I did not want to go, it was late-ish, I was tired, and I was spent. Whatever the Lord had in mind, couldn't it wait?

I shared with the Lord my need for rest and that He must have someone else that can go. He asked again, and once again; I declined. Then it happened...a huge internal disturbance, not spiritually but physically. All of a sudden I had a desire to go to the restroom. I knew if I did not go immediately I was going to need to clean my car on the inside.

I drove for a few more Miami blocks, and I felt as if I had been driving an eternity. I had to hold on; I had to find a restroom; and then I saw it. Big bright lights, a crowded parking lot, a familiar place; the book store! So I made a left turn and pulled into the parking lot. A car right at the entrance pulled out, and I thanked God for small mercies. The need to find a restroom was intense; as I pulled up and stepped out of the car, the thought of securing my car was the least of my concerns. I walked in to a Friday night frenzy; everyone seemed to be buying books. I asked the Lord to please allow me to make it to the restroom. It was at the back of the store, a long way off and with every step I took I thought I would have an accident right there and then.

I was stepping carefully, and I knew I was grimacing. It must have looked weird, and my imagination played with the idea that everyone was staring at me. I finally neared the bathroom; I could see the doors. To my right was a rest area where people sat and spoke; some read and others waited for friends. There were two comfy chairs that everyone liked to sit in; that is where I first saw him. He was sitting in one chair, and surprisingly the other was empty. He looked about 55, with a graying beard and long hair. He saw me as I was walking, our eyes met, and I nodded. He just looked at me and nodded back. I passed him, walking quickly. The bathroom was near; I was almost there...

Chapter 1

Wait…created in *whose* image?

"A spiritual revelation is nothing without an *internal* revolution…" My Mom.

I stared at myself in the mirror, not blinking, literally reflecting on who I thought I was. Deep down in my spirit, I knew there had to be more. I had to be more than the sum of my life experiences. I found myself often cogitating on the initial relationship with God and man. Questions and images flashed back and forth in my mind. What was it like to be the first man created? What was it like to be placed into a newly created body and take that first breath? Can you imagine seeing your Creator face-to-face? What was it like to be clothed in His anointing? What awestruck reverent wonder! Imagine the joy on their faces! What kind of relationship would I have had with my Father, the Creator of the universe? Why was that personal Father-son relationship eluding me? What did I need to abandon to achieve the purity of the same personal relationship that Jesus Christ had with His Father while on earth? I wanted answers. I needed answers.

Foundationally, I had to come to terms with what and who man really was. I was implanted with the illusion by my parents and the education system that my identity was in my skin color or my ethnic background. I was sold into the slavery mindset that my mirror image was who I actually was. I was under the impression that I was this body (flesh). For some time, I even thought I was a soul (my mind). Then one day I stepped into God's Reality. The very thing darkness did not want me to find out was revealed. It is in this revelation that I first found my freedom. It is in the understanding of what and who I am that I was able to walk closer with my Father. It is in this revelation that I was freed from my past and healed from so many hurts. I had an internal revolution. Here is where I came to know Reality. Here is where I realized what the Lord had wanted with Adam from the beginning. This was His initial intent.

For years, I had studied the Bible, read books, joined Bible studies, led in ministry, volunteered, and held concerts, dinners, and seminars. I was seen as an expert, a pastor, and teacher. I have come to understand that, at that time, I was totally oblivious to Reality and that there was so much more to grasp. I existed from a lot of information but survived without true revelation. I had knowledge of the written Word, and could even quote with the best of them, but I was missing that one thing. The one thing Christ was trying to share with every born-again believer. The Reality of how this Life in Christ is to be walked out.

As I was studying the Gospel of John, I noticed a reoccurring theme. Even though it is conspicuous throughout the Bible, this theme is interwoven in John's Gospel like a golden thread. It is never more obvious than in chapter 4 when the Lord was speaking to the woman at the well. The woman dialogued with Christ regarding the proper location of where the Lord God of Israel should be worshipped: was it on the mountain or in the Temple? The Lord made a matter of fact statement. He answered her by stating: "God is a Spirit: and they that worship him must worship him in spirit and in truth" (John 4:24 KJV).

"God is a Spirit (a spiritual Being) and those who worship Him must worship Him in spirit and in truth (reality)" (John 4:24 AMP).

Now this led me to seek an answer from Holy Spirit. I asked myself "If God is Spirit, if I can only worship Him in 'spirit' and truth (Reality), is there a spiritual place I need to go to? And if God is Spirit, and I am made in His Image, what does that make me?" **After all, flesh and spirit are not the same thing.** As I started to search these things out, Holy Spirit led me to the "beginning."

"And God said, Let us make man in **our image**, after **our likeness:** and let them have dominion over the fish of the sea, and over the fowl of the air, and over the cattle, and over all the earth, and over every creeping thing that creepeth upon the earth" (Genesis 1:26 KJV, emphasis added).

These words rang through my soul-realm (mind) over and over again. How often had I read this and just glossed over it? *"Our image…Our Likeness…"* Now please do not get ahead of me. It is not the words that I italicized above that make me stop in my tracks, but reading them after reading John 4:24, in light of knowing that God is Spirit. That is what made me stop, sit up and take notice and look into more literal translations.

"Then God said, 'Let us make a man —**someone like ourselves**, to be the master of all life upon the earth and in the skies and in the seas' " (Genesis 1:26 TLB, emphasis added).

"God is sheer being itself—Spirit. Those who worship him must do it out of their very being, their spirits, their true selves, in adoration" (John 4:24 MSG).

"For God is Spirit, so those who worship him must worship in spirit and in truth" (John 4:24 NLT).

"God is a Spirit (a spiritual Being) and those who worship Him must worship Him in spirit and in truth (reality)" (John 4:24 AMP).

God is Spirit, and even though many have read this far in this book and thought, "Well yeah, duh! I know that!" I wonder how many know what that means for them. Dear reader, there has to be more to this life than what I saw in the mirror this morning. After all man was Created in God's Image, and His very likeness. Right?

Then, it dawned on me that man is spirit, period. A spiritual being, and totally separate from flesh and from the soul. There has to be a different life to live than how I had been living it. There had to be one Truth, one Way, and one Life.

I pursued revelation on these things. The revelation came with a message that left me uncomfortable in the flesh. It became apparent to me that I had been engaged with many steps in church; like the twelve steps to this, and eight steps to that, and not one of the step programs were getting me closer to God. On the contrary, they made me feel good in my flesh but kept me estranged from Him in what mattered; spirit. I just knew something was missing. These steps were not worth stepping into if they were not leading me closer to God.

While in prayer one day, Holy Spirit shared with me that my formula was backwards. Many modern day churches (not all churches so please don't send emails) preach and follow a "plan" in the flesh that does not fall in line with God's original intent for Adam.

Speaking of myself and my own experience; I was brought into a church, and immediately (or eventually) was asked to serve. I was placed in a men's group or small group and shortly thereafter, due to my "knowledge" of the Bible and due to my zeal for wanting to "grow", I was made a leader. I was kept busy, and in that busyness I remained immature, my growth in spirit, as His son, was stunted due to my focus on acts rather than Him. I found myself getting older in the body but not maturing in spirit. The truth is that I never knew how to show my growth other than "doing" things and "showing" how much Bible I knew. I dismally confused these for true relationship with God.

I grew in Outer Court (worldly) recognition and in my flesh I felt a sense of accomplishment. I grew in "knowledge," my ability to get scripture together and do studies, which helped my soul (mind) grow and provided preaching experience, etc.

I had been saved and born again for a long time, and was still retarded when it came to knowing and hearing from God. The definition of retarded is "to delay or slow down (the progress, speed, or development) of (something)" (Collins English Dictionary).

Due to my own lack of understanding and my exposure to poor teaching I was not maturing into Christ-likeness. My TRUE spiritual growth was stunted, retarded, delayed. I was still on milk and spiritually anemic. I was in the "church body" for over 20 years and still trapped in a darkened prison of my mind due to poor teaching, religious tradition, and lack of relationship with God due to *my own* dis-obedience to His Truth. Yet this is not a condemnation rant, I am just being transparent with my location in Christ (or lack of) at that moment. This kept me in the church body and out of the Body of Christ. These are two very different bodies.

I sincerely believe some are reading this and can relate to being overwhelmed in ministry service. At times, you may have felt stressed out or even frustrated in your growth, and especially in "doing" ministry; what is about to follow is written for you. It is just as possible that you are on the other spectrum. You feel wonderful; service is easy and never a bother; as a matter of fact you never felt more alive or useful than when you are serving. What is about to follow is especially for you. If there is anyone in between these two extremes, pay close attention because this is definitely for you.

Letting God overwrite my programming

What I am about to share are some of the basic things my Father has asked me to share with His children. I usually prefer to share with new believers. There seems to be a lot less detoxing from religious addictions they may have and minimal reprogramming of incorrect doctrine that has corrupted their spiritual hard-drives like a virus. However, newly saved or veteran the following is vital to our walk.

There is one distinction that is paramount to our maturing in Christ; knowing you ARE spirit and not just as someone who "has" a spirit. "God is Spirit" (John 4:24 NKJV). Obviously, if we are made in His image AFTER we are born-again through accepting Jesus Christ as our Lord of all and Savior, then we are born again; in and as *spirit*. We were made for the purpose of true worship and real relationship with Him; spiritually as spiritual beings, in His Reality.

This leads then to one of several questions. If man is spirit; what was formed from the dust of the ground? Obviously they are not the same thing. Spirit is spirit created by God; flesh, on the other hand, is dust; the flesh was made by God from something that was here on earth. What's the difference? The next chapters clear this up. Some believers are under the misconception they are flesh, and spirit is something that we "will be" in Heaven. I believed that also, once.

Understanding you are not flesh but spirit and live *in* a body is a good revelation, but looking God, by walking in spirit, only comes after a long revolution.

Chapter 2

What is man? Understanding how we were Created

"...touch Me and see, for a spirit does not have flesh and bones..." Jesus Christ (Luke 24:39 NASB)

Without the revelation of our true identity in the new birth, a Christian cannot walk out all that God has for them. The first three chapters of the book of Genesis are crucial to understanding God's original intent for man. I slowed down when I was studying these scriptures and asked Holy Spirit to lead me. I did not want to read it from an area of familiarity; therefore, I am asking you to read with me these scriptures anew and follow carefully in Christ. Amen?

When God created Man, He created Man as spirit ***and then*** He made the flesh. Realizing this leads to a freedom in Christ that is Heavenly. Pay close attention.

There are three words being translated for "created," "made," and "formed" in Genesis. In the English language, they all seem the same; yet understanding the meaning of the aforementioned three words is key to unlocking many insights into who and what we are. The words may appear relatively similar in English, but in Hebrew they are different.

Bara' (Strong's Hebrew Concordance #1254)

We first look at the word bara', a verb that is mainly used in reference to God and His Work alone (Genesis 1:1 and 1:21). Bara' represents a God type of Creation that brings into being something that has never been seen before. It is best recognizable in Genesis 1:1, When Holy Spirit moved Moses to write; God "created" the Heavens and the earth. Speakers of Hebrew understand that it means "out of nothing." One instant it did not exist; God spoke; it was manifested.

Bible scholars recognize this as the explanation of creation phrase in Latin known as *ex nihilo* or literally translated, "out of nothing." When you hear your Pastor or someone say the world was fashioned ex nihilo (created from nothing that existed), this is made possible by the understanding of the word bara'.

Let me share an illustration. Let's make believe that I spoke into being a talking butterfly with a dragon-like tail that ate lemons. Now we all know that no such thing exists, nor can I speak that into being... but if it just "appeared" from thin air. Poof! Voila! It is there. Flying about and chewing on a lemon. Well that brethren would be bara' at work. In the same way, man did not exist until God spoke and man was created. Man was "created" out of nothing, in the image of God, spirit. "So God created [**bara'**] man in His own image, in the image and likeness of God He created [**bara'**] him; male and female He created [**bara'**] them" (Genesis 1:27 AMP, emphasis and "**bara'**" added).

Asa (Strong's Hebrew Concordance #6213)

The second word we will look at is asa. Asa means more of "the work" involved in the forming from something that already exists." An action; Genesis 1:26 clearly states that God said let us "make" (asa) man. One could assume that man is no different from the animals. Review verse 25 and you will find the same verb used for the "beasts of the earth." Until you get to verse 27 and the assumption is ended. The verb bara' describes man being Created (bara') in God's own Image from nothing that pre-existed. God CREATES (bara') animate life in Genesis 1:21 and then goes about in the action/work of making (asa) living creatures from this new life He created. God created (bara') a life, and then from that life He made (asa) more of the same.

The Hebrew verbs bara' and asa obviously are not the same. Bara' means "to create" and in the Pentateuch, is normally speaking of God's creative power. Asa is never translated as "create" in the King James Bible, but it can refer to a creative *act* as described in Genesis 1:31 and Genesis 2:2.

I will share an earthly example: If I made (asa) you a cotton sweater. I may have made (asa) the cotton sweater (knitted, sewed, etc.) out of cotton because it (cotton) already existed, however, I did not create (bara') cotton itself. The sweater was made (asa) from something already created (bara'). In this case, cotton. So while I may have made you the sweater I "made" (asa) it from something that already existed, we agree that cotton already existed, right? My action or work to make the sweater is "asa."

God created from nothing, a special being, one created in His own Image and His own Likeness; spirit. A spiritual being and God named that being Adam. Now the "work" that was done to make man is "asa." The speaking itself is an action, the making, "asa."

God *created* man as spirit, but for man to function on earth, he (man) would need one thing. What was it? Before I give you the answer, I must share with you the third Hebrew word we need to go over in Genesis.

Yāṣar (Strong's Hebrew Concordance #3335)

Yāṣar, like asa, deals with the "making" of something, but it steps up the action. It means more than the work involved in asa "to make" something. This word takes on a special implication of a Personal Touch. Its origin lies in the ideas of cutting and framing with intention and with purpose (Strong's Hebrew Concordance #3335). Imagine the work of a potter, a writer, a blacksmith, working on a project with a specific end in mind. A potter knows what the vessel is for before he even begins the work. "What are you working on?" A passerby may ask the potter. "A water pot." the potter replies. Or a wine jug, or vase. When the potter sat down to do the work and form this vessel he knew what it was to hold. Yāṣar gives the impression of something being formed with a reason. This word describes deliberate action in the Garden of Eden with forethought by God Himself. The word leaves no place for any idea of accidental or haphazard works. When you think yāṣar, imagine God as a potter, not just forming a vessel, but forming the vessel and knowing it has a purpose BEFORE it is done.

Please take a minute and answer the following questions:
- If you were on the moon, what kind of suit would you need to function there?

- If you were working underwater what kind of suit would you need?

Well the answers respectively are; spacesuit, and scuba suit. These are suits that allow our body to function in an environment that it was not created for. These are suits I PUT ON; I am in and part of the suit, yet, I am not *the* suit.

So what suit would I need as spirit, to function on earth?

I would need an "earth-suit." A suit that allows me (spirit) to function on earth. A suit formed (yāṣar) of the same material this earth is made out of. A suit that allows me to interact with this material world, even though I am created in my Father's image as spirit. An earth-suit was formed for Adam to function and interact with this world and to have dominion over it. In the joining of flesh and spirit, man became a living soul (mind). Please be aware that the spark of life came from man (spirit) being breathed into the earth-suit, not the other way around.

Why does a potter make a wine jug? Because wine already exists, it needs to be poured into something that can hold it. Why does a potter make a water jug? To hold water; water came first and THEN the water jug. Why did God form (yāṣar) an earth-suit for man? Because man is spirit; man needed a vessel to be poured into so he could interact with the things on this planet. (Remember, we are in this world but not of it.) He needed an earth-suit to make him compatible in a world that was not made of spirit material. God created (bara') man from nothing. In His working to make (asa) man functional on this planet, He placed man into a body He formed (**yāṣar**) and fashioned with intimate details and attention from the very dust of the Earth. The spirit-man that God placed into the body of dust is what gave it Life. "And the LORD God formed [**yāṣar**] man *of* the dust of the ground, and breathed into his nostrils the breath of life; **and man became a living soul**" (Genesis 2:7 KJV, emphasis and "**yāṣar**" added).

"Then the Lord God formed man from the dust of the ground and breathed into his nostrils the breath *or* spirit of life, and man became a living being" (Genesis 2:7 AMP).

As Holy Spirit led me, I wrote a fictional story to illustrate the word yāṣar and the work of "forming" of man's body.

What if you were a witness in God's workshop on the sixth day of creation? You witness Him taking dust from the earth and forming a vessel. He knits intricate and complex connections.

Patiently he molds each socket, with loving attention He softens the surface. All the angles and connecting areas are smoothed with a Master's eye. He is focused on every last atom. He counts every hair and strengthens every bone. He is about His work with a Father's Love.

Quietly you ask, "Lord, what are you forming?"

"An earth-suit," He replies without taking His eyes from His work.

Amazed at His artistic greatness and mesmerized by His integrity to detail, you lean in to take in more of His handiwork. Your heart beats faster, and you marvel at one overt fact; the same hand that molded mountains and carved out valleys; that weighed the earth and set the sun, that same hand that holds the universe was forming another piece of art, and yet you sense a difference. What was it? Then it dawns on you; it is not just the vessel that is different but God's intense focus on this vessel. The gleam in His eye when He picks it up and examines it; the smile on His face as He moves each part one at a time as if controlling the quality of His own work. You try not to gaze for too long, but your eyes cannot pull away. You realize that He is forming something special; something close to His heart…what could its purpose be?

"Lord, what is the purpose of this beautiful work?" You inquire.

He raises His eyes momentarily and looks off to the corner. You follow His gaze, and it is only then that you notice him. Until that moment, you were unaware of another presence there. At first you thought it was because the Lord's Glory filled the room that you were not aware of this being. Comprehension of the truth slowly sets in; God's Glory was only part of the reason this presence was not made known to you. The creation in the corner resembled God Himself, spirit. It had His image and was in His likeness. They were so similar that they seemed to be a part of each other.

You look back at the Lord with a raised eyebrow, and He answers the question in your heart before you speak. "This is Adam; I am forming a vessel to pour Adam into it. He will have dominion over the earth and move in my Glory, Grace and Power. I desire a relationship with him as he is; spirit, but he needs this vessel to function appropriately in this kingdom called earth I am gifting to him."

You sit and wait to see it all work out, digesting the

information, trying to wrap your own understanding around what you just heard and what you are seeing. Then with a satisfied smile God gets up from His chair, and you know it is finished. With an ever so gentle move, He picks up the vessel in one hand and with the other He lifts Adam. With one breath, Adam is injected into the vessel. The vessel is set down, and there is an instant spark, an obvious internal explosion. The chest expands with breath and the eyes blink with recognition as they look upon the Lord. The limbs move and instinctually perform their first action; Adam bends his knee and bows his head. Then he speaks his first words in the earth-suit "My Father, thank you."

The Lord is smiling, like a new Father beholding His baby for the first time. As they walk off in the cool of the day you hear the Lord say, "All of this is yours" as His hand gestures across the length of the horizon. "Father, why do I need this …this…body? Why can I not just be in my natural state?" Adam asks with the innocence of a child. "The Lord's answer seems to make the sky become clearer; the sun shine brighter, and the flowers become more fragrant. He said "I have given you this planet as your kingdom. If you were to stay as spirit, well then you would not be King in the spirit realm my son, For I Am King and I alone am Lord for I Am all and all is what I AM. You will learn to be like me on earth, you will fellowship with me as you create this world into a replica of My Kingdom. You will make more like yourself, and we will teach them to be kings and lords here on earth, but I shall be King of kings and Lord of lords. I shall be your God, and I shall be your Father. You shall all be my sons, and we will fellowship eternally."

That is when it dawns on you, everything around you, everything you could see, all that had been made, formed or created was for Adam. You cannot help, but smile, it is obvious for all to see this is the beginning of a Love affair unlike no other. This will be the greatest Love story ever told. Amen.

I pray you enjoyed reading my fictional story as much as I enjoyed writing it. The purpose was not just to move you with a story, but to assist in your understanding that without man (spirit) that the body would not have known Life; there would have been no spark in the body, and no godly purpose. After all, God created man in His image and His likeness, as spirit. His purpose though, is to have man enjoy Heaven on earth; to walk like God and have authority like God and live an anointed life here on earth as His sons and daughters. "God said, Let Us [Father, Son, and Holy Spirit] make mankind in Our image, after Our likeness, **and let them have complete authority** over the fish of the sea, the birds of the air, the [tame] beasts, *__and over all of the earth__*, and over everything that creeps upon the earth" (Genesis 1:26 AMP, emphasis added).

To live on this earth, we need an earth-suit to move around as "earthly" kings. But we are spirit. Do not confuse your flesh with who you really are. While it is true that, as a result of our fallen nature, we deal with our flesh daily and due to the flesh and mind not being born-again; we have two natures that fight against each other (Galatians 5:17). I can only speak for myself; I deal with my old self daily; however, there is one fact to remember; this body NEEDS my spirit to function. My spirit does not need this body to be alive. "For as the human body apart from the spirit is lifeless, so faith apart from [its] works of obedience is also dead" (James 2:26 AMP).

There is a good chance that while you are reading this you are wearing clothes. You and the clothes are technically one. I mean, if I poked the shirt you are wearing right now with a sharp long needle, it would be a safe bet that your body would get pierced also. Right? Yet you are in your clothes, but you are NOT your clothes. In the same way, you ARE spirit. You wear an earth-suit (body), but you are not actually that body. If you were looking at me right now you could see my flesh, my earth-suit, but you are not really seeing me, spirit. You are just seeing what I am dressed in.

Here let me provide more scripture about Man, being spirit. These are but a few:

__We understand God through spirit__

"But *there is* a spirit in man: and the inspiration of the Almighty giveth them understanding" (Job 32:8 KJV).

"But there is [a vital force] a spirit [of intelligence] in man, and the breath of the Almighty gives men understanding" (Job 32:8 AMP).

"But it is not mere age that makes men wise. Rather, it is the spirit in a man, the breath of the Almighty that makes him intelligent" (Job 32:8 TLB).

"But there is a spirit within people, the breath of the Almighty within them, that makes them intelligent" (Job 32:8 NLT).

"But it is the spirit in a man, the breath of the Almighty, that gives him understanding" (Job 32:8 NIV).

Spirit is inside the body

"THE BURDEN *or* oracle (the thing to be lifted up) of the word of the Lord concerning Israel: Thus says the Lord, Who stretches out the heavens and lays the foundation of the earth and forms the spirit of man within him:" (Zechariah 12:1 AMP).

"This is the fate of Israel, as pronounced by the Lord, who stretched out the heavens, laid the foundation of the earth, and formed the spirit of man within him:" (Zechariah 12:1 TLB).

"War Bulletin: GOD's Message concerning Israel, GOD's Decree—the very GOD who threw the skies into space, set earth on a firm foundation, and breathed his own life into men and women:" (Zechariah 12:1 MSG).

"The burden of a word of Jehovah on Israel. An affirmation of Jehovah, Stretching out heaven, and founding earth, And forming the spirit of man in his midst" (Zechariah 12:1 YLT).

"This is the word of the LORD concerning Israel. The LORD, who stretches out the heavens, who lays the foundation of the earth, and who forms the spirit of man within him, declares:" (Zechariah 12:1 NIV).

When we die we go back to God as spirit!

"Then shall the dust return to the earth as it was: and the spirit shall return unto God who gave it" (Ecclesiastes 12:7 KJV).

"Then shall the dust [out of which God made man's body] return to the earth as it was, and the spirit shall return to God Who gave it" (Ecclesiastes 12:7 AMP).

"We are confident, *I say*, and willing rather to be absent from the body, and to be present with the Lord" (2 Corinthians 5:8 KJV).

"[Yes] we have confident *and* hopeful courage and are pleased rather to be away from home out of the body and be at home with the Lord" (2 Corinthians 5:8 AMP).

"We are confident, I say, and would prefer to be away from the body and at home with the Lord" (2 Corinthians 5:8 NIV).

It is in spirit that we get revelations

"The spirit of man *is* the candle of the LORD, searching all the inward parts of the belly" (Proverbs 20:27 KJV).

"The spirit of man [that factor in human personality which proceeds immediately from God] is the lamp of the Lord, searching all his innermost parts" (Proverbs 20:27 AMP).

God speaks to us through Holy Spirit and our spirit

"The Spirit itself beareth witness with our spirit, that we are the children of God" (Romans 8:16 KJV).

"The Spirit Himself [thus] testifies together with our own spirit, [assuring us] that we are children of God" (Romans 8:16 AMP).

"The Spirit himself testifies with our spirit that we are God's children" (Romans 8:16 NIV).

We are joined to the Lord in spirit

"But he that is joined unto the Lord is one spirit" (1 Corinthians 6:17 KJV).

"But the person who is united to the Lord becomes one spirit with Him" (1 Corinthians 6:17 AMP).

"For what man knoweth the things of a man, save the spirit of man which is in him? even so the things of God knoweth no man, but the Spirit of God" (1 Corinthians 2:11 KJV).

"For what person perceives (knows and understands) what passes through a man's thoughts except the man's own spirit within him? Just so no one discerns (comes to know and comprehend) the thoughts of God except the Spirit of God" (1 Corinthians 2:11 AMP).

God is what? And I worship Him HOW?

"God is Spirit. And those that worship Him must do so in spirit and in truth" (John 4:24 KJV).

Spirit has nothing to do with flesh and bones...body

"Behold my hands and my feet, that it is I myself: handle me, and see; for a spirit hath not flesh and bones, as ye see me have" (Luke 24:39 KJV).

"See My hands and My feet, that it is I Myself! Feel *and* handle Me and see, for a spirit does not have flesh and bones, as you see that I have" (Luke 24:39 AMP).

You are spirit. You live in a body. But if your body were to expire right now, and you are a born-again believer, you would be present with the Lord-alive! We are not discussing flesh but spirit. Your body NEEDS you (spirit) to live; you do not need your body (flesh). You are spirit, created by God Himself.

The Lord speaking to Nicodemus about the new birth said: "That which is born of the flesh is flesh; [**our body**] and that which is born of the Spirit is spirit" [**me/spirit**] (John 3:6 KJV, emphasis and bracketed words added).

"What is born of [from] the flesh is flesh [of the physical is physical]; and what is born of the Spirit is spirit" (John 3:6 AMP).

"Flesh gives birth to flesh, but the Spirit gives birth to spirit" (John 3:6 NIV).

Flesh gives birth to flesh and Spirit (with a capital "S," meaning Holy Spirit) gives birth to spirit. When I was born again, I was born in and as spirit; a baby at that. Holy Spirit came at that moment, and I was transformed. My old me passed away; I was reborn, made brand new! It was my lack of understanding of this one factor that kept me spiritually retarded for years. I was a slave to a dead person (the old me that has passed away) because I did not understand growing up INTO the new birth.

This is a Truth that has to be revealed. As long as you are looking at yourself as flesh or the sum of knowledge you have attained through your past, your growth will stay in an infantile state regardless of what you know or how long you have been in the church. This brings us to the next part, a very crucial part. Many Christians are under the false impression that spirit and soul are the same. Not true. One can look and sound good, but only the spirit when led by Holy Spirit can look, sound and act God.

Chapter 3

Not sold out, but being "souled" out...

"If you know your enemy and yourself, you will not be at risk in a hundred battles." Sun Tzu

Man is spirit; he has a soul and lives in a body. Weird thing to hear, huh? Until you become aware of whom God created you to be, you are stuck in thinking you are that person in the mirror, or you are your upbringing, culture, or color of your flesh, etc. Once He gives you the revelation of whom and what you really are, then it is obvious, there is no other way around it. True freedom begins to manifest.

When the Lord blessed me with this revelation and gave me understanding, my walk became more loving. I am now more forgiving, and I am able to listen to Holy Spirit clearer and with a new sense of wonder. These are a few results of getting to know my true identity.

First things first. Let's take a look at what the Word of God says about spirit, soul and body. "And the very God of peace sanctify you wholly; and *I pray God* your **whole spirit** and **soul** and **body** be preserved blameless unto the coming of our Lord Jesus Christ" (1 Thessalonians 5:23 KJV).

"And may the God of peace Himself sanctify you through and through [separate you from profane things, make you pure and wholly consecrated to God]; and may your **spirit** and **soul** and **body** be preserved sound *and* complete [and found] blameless at the coming of our Lord Jesus Christ (the Messiah)" (1 Thessalonians 5:23 AMP).

"May the God of peace himself make you entirely pure and devoted to God; and may your **spirit and soul and body** be kept strong and blameless until that day when our Lord Jesus Christ comes back again" (1 Thessalonians 5:23 TLB).

"May God himself, the God of peace, sanctify you through and through. May your **whole spirit, soul and body** be kept blameless at the coming of our Lord Jesus Christ" (1 Thessalonians 5:23 NIV).

Holy Spirit speaking through the Apostle gives us a clear picture of our own triune make-up: God is three in one, Father, Son and Holy Spirit. We function the same way; we are spirit; we have a soul and live in a body. According to scripture, man is spirit. We also know the Lord fashioned an earth-suit that we call a body and we function on earth through this body.

Now, what is a soul? The soul is the meeting point between spirit and body; the connector, it acts like a phone line. We can only worship God in spirit. So in a perfect world I speak to, fellowship with and worship God. My spirit (lowercase "s") is submissive to the Spirit of God in me (Holy Spirit). The soul (mind) is supposed to be submissive to me as I walk in and am led in spirit, and then the body does as the soul (mind) dictates since the flesh does as we think. The soul (mind) plays an important part in my daily walk. "For as he [man] thinks in his heart, so is he" (Proverbs 23:7 NKJV). We need to be mindful of our thoughts. Are they my Father God's thoughts, or thoughts of a past life influenced by darkness and the devil?

As long as both myself (spirit) and Holy Spirit are in union and I choose to obey His promptings, I control my soul (mind) through obeying Holy Spirit and getting my soul (mind) to submit. Then the body follows along. I am living a God life because Holy Spirit will only lead me on God paths.

So, why do we struggle so much with obeying God? Unfortunately, my soul and body are un-regenerated. They still have the programming prior to my accepting Christ, the programming of the world, the ideas of darkness, opinions based on my own self-values, experiences and bias views. Yes, my soul realm has decades of experience, and it is well developed. That is where the battle is; for control of my soul. Whoever the soul is being controlled by will be manifested by the body in words and deeds.

Let's say I asked you to raise your hand right now, and you did it. The soul (mind) is the one that told the body to raise its hand; the body follows what it is told to do by the soul (mind). When my soul (mind) is being controlled by my obedience to Holy Spirit my body will do as it is told and not what it wants to or was trained to do in a past life; therefore becoming a living sacrifice (Romans 12:1).

Listening to Holy Spirit can only be done in spirit.

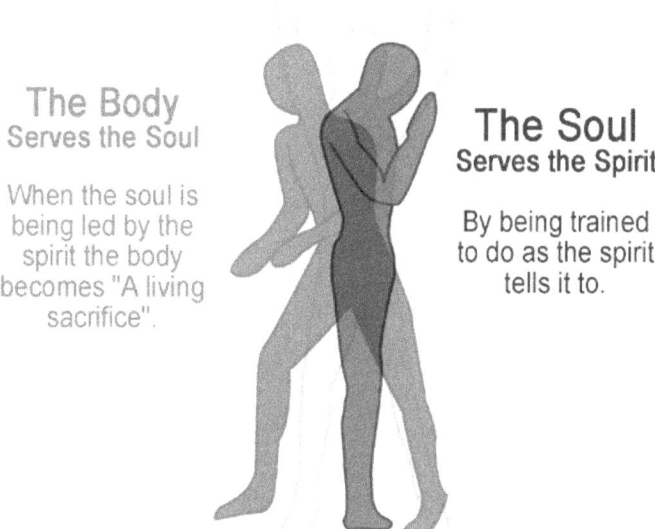

The Body
Serves the Soul

When the soul is being led by the spirit the body becomes "A living sacrifice".

The Soul
Serves the Spirit

By being trained to do as the spirit tells it to.

God's intent in my new birth is that I serve God (as I communicate with Holy Spirit in me); my soul should serve me (spirit), and the body should be obedient to the soul. Perfect; Christ-like.

The spirit and the soul are very close, but they are not the same thing. "For the word of God *is* quick, and powerful, and sharper than any two edged sword, piercing even to the **dividing** asunder of **soul and spirit**, and of the joints and marrow, and *is* a discerner of the thoughts and intents of the heart" (Hebrews 4:12 KJV, emphasis added).

"For the word of God is living and active. Sharper than any double-edged sword, it penetrates even to **dividing soul and spirit, joints and marrow; it judges the thoughts and attitudes of the heart**" (Hebrews 4:12 NIV, emphasis added).

In the New Testament, we have two words generally used for "mind." The first word is: "nous" meaning mind or thoughts (Strong's Greek Concordance #3563). The second word is "psyche" and is used as soul 58 times (Strong's Greek Concordance #5590).

The words psychology and psychiatry are derived from "**psyche**," also known as the study and the healing of the **mind**. The soul is where I have my emotions, feelings, attitudes; you can say my "personality." It is not, however, who I am. I am a spiritual creation; I have a soul (mind), and I live in a body (flesh). It is in spirit that I was born- again. It is in spirit that God is raising me. It is in spirit that I will become Christ-like. Yet in me, I have a soul that is opposed to that one very thing. And the transformation of my soul/mind is the key to my growth.

The words "**dividing soul and spirit**" used in Hebrews 4:12 are **psyche** for the word soul; this is the word we derive psychiatry and psychology from while **pneuma** is the word we use for spirit (Strong's Greek Concordance # 4151). There is a clear distinction.

Transformed ... like a butterfly

"Do not **be conformed to this world** (this age), [fashioned after and adapted to its external, superficial customs], but be transformed (changed) by the [entire] renewal of **your mind** [by its new ideals and its new attitude], so that you may prove [for yourselves] what is the good and acceptable and perfect will of God, *even* the thing which is good and acceptable and perfect [in His sight for you]" (Romans 12:2 AMP, emphasis added).

The word here for "transform" in Greek is metamorphoō. The same word we get metamorphosis from. It is the process a caterpillar goes through in order to emerge as a butterfly. I am to transform my thoughts and beliefs on a daily basis to that which resembles Christ. I was already born-again as spirit, but it takes a daily effort to be transformed by following Holy Spirit rather than the familiar paths of my old life. It is in this transformation that we find the training to becoming more and more Christ-like. Like a caterpillar, I have to be ready to die and give up my old life of being confined to this planet so that God can transform me into His beautiful creation; as a son, resembling Him flying above earthly circumstances (Isaiah 40:31).

Apostle Paul shares in Romans 12:1-2, two things: first, that I make my body an acceptable sacrifice (Romans 12:1). Using the word sacrifice lets me know that my body may not be inclined to do what the Lord wants it to do. Actually, as soon as I get a word from the Lord through Holy Spirit and I focus on walking it out; my flesh (body) will be opposed to anything God wants of me. (Galatians 5:17). And secondly, that I am not to conform to what I see the world doing and by what this age *thinks* is appropriate. Instead, I am to be transformed by the total renewing of my mind (Romans 12:2). This makes me aware that it (my mind/my soul) has ideas and thoughts that ARE NOT of my Father. This mind needs to be renewed!

God is asking for a total transformation, like a caterpillar into a butterfly. A new way of getting around, a new perspective, a lighter load; no longer confined to eating the dusty dictates of this world whose god is satan. Instead, I am to fly along a current of air called Holy Spirit, and this current that is in me yet also outside of me will guide me to my specific plant to give me the nectar I need to live. Just like a caterpillar moves from one plant to another plant, I live from grace to grace.

The renewing of my mind is an integral part of maturity. This is where the Christian needs to make a decision, either sell out to the world and follow the world's way of doing things, or become **souled** out to God by listening to Holy Spirit and following His promptings. The latter, however, can only be done in and through Christ's grace.

In this one area, I seem to fail the most. It has been a learning curve. It has taken daily battles between spirit and soul. It has required me to shut out all things but my Father's voice. I had to get serious about my walk. Many times I have been called to "sell-out" my faith by darkness. My daily prayer always includes *"Lord when I am put to the test today let me answer in You as spirit and not bend my will to those thoughts that were preprogrammed by my old self in darkness. By Your grace Lord, I will resist and triumph in Your power."*

My soul realm (my mind) was trained up by darkness through movies, television, books, magazines, past hurts, childhood issues, parental issues, lost loved ones, affiliations with my skin's color, dependency on my "knowledge," my abilities, my self-dependence, etc. These things have not been reborn. The Word of God tells us:

"[Inasmuch as we] refute arguments *and* theories *and*

reasonings and every proud *and* lofty thing that sets itself up against the [true] knowledge of God; and we lead every thought *and* purpose away captive into the obedience of Christ (the Messiah, the Anointed One)" (2 Corinthians 10:5 AMP).

Following my own ideas and leaning on my own understanding is a familiar place to be. MY thoughts are good thoughts and MY ways seem to have worked out in the past (sometimes), and after all, I did go to school for this and that…why do I need to check with God? Yes, this was my mantra for so many years. Dependence on self, church and others was the norm. Depending only on God and building a relationship through Holy Spirit, on the other hand, is actually my destiny. I must step away from the familiar to get closer to the Father.

One looks good to the world. One receives plaudits and recognition. One makes me out to be smart, witty, productive, and helpful, a "server." The other in its quiet outward manifestations of an internal transformation just looks God.

Chapter 4

The bending of my ME…

"Father, if you are willing, take this cup from me; yet not my will, but yours be done." Jesus Christ
(Luke 22:42 NIV)

The flesh (my body) is the last part of this tri-unity. I am spirit; I have a soul, and I live in a body. Granted, my mind and my body are a part of me. Like my hair, eye color and skin tone, I live with them. I am aware that my mind and flesh have their own desires, nature and agendas. They have their own appetites and hungers. They have a preprogrammed path to follow, but I cannot allow them to; for those things of the flesh are against my very Life as a spirit being. The flesh interferes with my growth into Christ-likeness.

"For those who are according to the flesh *and* are controlled by its unholy desires set their minds on *and* pursue those things which gratify the flesh, but those who are according to the Spirit *and* are controlled by the desires of the Spirit set their minds on *and* seek those things which gratify the [Holy] Spirit" (Romans 8:5 AMP).

The scriptures state that as a born again believer, I am not to live a fleshly lifestyle.

"But you are not living the life of the flesh, you are living the life of the Spirit, if the [Holy] Spirit of God [really] dwells within you [directs and controls you]…." (Romans 8:9a AMP).

I knew this intellectually, but not from experience. What was wrong with me? Why could I not control this flesh?

I was praying every morning; I was part of the prayer group, and I was reading the Word, yet, I felt that there was more. There seemed to be something that was missing. One day I thought I heard the Lord say "Bend your *knee*."

I replied, "Really, Lord? I do bend my knee; I prostrate; I lay out. How much lower can I get?"

He answered: "Not your *knee*, your ME."

It became obvious that there was something in ME that was getting in the way. What I found out about myself is priceless. It was life changing and ME breaking. I had been born-again, in spirit yet living like the old man that passed away. The word says: "Therefore if any person is [ingrafted] in Christ (the Messiah) he is a new creation (a new creature altogether); the old [previous moral and spiritual condition] has passed away. Behold, the fresh *and* new has come!" (2 Corinthians 5:17 AMP).

I have a new nature. Obviously with a new nature comes a new appetite, right? Yet I seemed to be doing the same things I was doing prior to being born-again. I was dependent on my gifting, my abilities, and my self-reliance. I knew how "this worked" and how "that was supposed to be." I felt that I knew it all, and now that I was on God's side I assumed He wanted me to use my knowledge to minister; He had much to teach me and I had much to learn.

Walking away from my former father

One of hardest things I ever had to come to terms with was the fact that I needed to be reprogrammed (and in MANY areas still do). This will be an on-going task until He returns; however, it does get better as we mature. My soul realm (mind) had been constantly programmed by darkness in my former life; by my former father, satan. I needed to un-program my soul (mind). My ways of doing things had to decrease, and Christ had to increase in me. After all, my Father's thoughts are not mine; His ways are not mine, but praise God, *He wants them to be!*

Now before you read too much into that preceding statement, understand that when we were not yet in Christ we were of satan. Ponder what Jesus said when He was speaking to the Pharisees. " 'You are of your father, the devil, and it is your will to practice the lusts *and* gratify the desires [which are characteristic] of your father. He was a murderer from the beginning and does not stand in the truth, because there is no truth in him. When he speaks a falsehood, he speaks what is natural to him, for he is a liar [himself] and the father of lies *and* of all that is false' " (John 8:44 AMP).

This was not just for those Pharisees. No, darkness works in all soul realms (minds). Let us take a look at a discussion between Jesus Christ and His twelve disciples. Jesus first asked His disciples who the "people" said He was. In other words, "What's the 411, what's the word on the street?"

"Now when Jesus went into the region of Caesarea Philippi, He asked His disciples, Who do people say that the Son of Man is?" (Matthew 16:13 AMP).

So they answered Him; ". . . some say John the Baptist; others say Elijah; and others Jeremiah or one of the prophets" (Matthew 16:14 AMP).

Christ, after hearing, who the "people" said He was, decided to narrow down the question. "He said to them, But who do you [yourselves] say that I am?" (Matthew 16:15 AMP).

In other words, now that we know what the "people" are saying…"who do **YOU** say I am?" (Matthew 16:15 NKJV).

"...Simon Peter replied, *You are the Christ, the Son of the living God.* Then Jesus answered him, blessed (happy, fortunate, and to be envied) are you, Simon Bar-Jonah. **For flesh and blood** [men] have not revealed this to you, but My Father Who is in heaven. And I tell you, you are Peter [Greek, *Petros*—a large piece of rock], and on this rock [Greek, *petra*—a huge rock like Gibraltar] [**your revelation**] I will build My church, and the gates of Hades (the powers of the infernal region) shall not overpower it [or be strong to its detriment or hold out against it]" (Matthew 16:15-18 AMP, emphasis and "your revelation" added).

Simon, son of Jonah, stepped up to the plate and was the first to acknowledge whom Christ was. Upon Simon sharing the revelation he had, the Lord said Simon was blessed because man did not tell him this but instead he had a direct revelation from Holy Spirit. He even gave him a new name; Peter. How exciting to know that revelation does not come through flesh or from flesh but only through God, Amen?!

But this is not the point here. Here is where it gets sticky. Soon after this revelation, where the Lord publicly gave Simon plaudits and a big pat on the back, Christ made this statement directly to him.

"But Jesus turned **away from Peter** and said **to him**, Get behind Me, **Satan**! You are in My way [an offense and a hindrance and a snare to Me]; **for you are minding what partakes not of the nature *and* quality of God, but of men**" (Matthew 16:23 AMP, emphasis added).

Why? What do you think caused the sudden change? How could the great Peter be so quickly reprimanded? Here is why. In verse 20-21, the Lord was explaining to His disciples what He (Christ) would have to go through, and Peter pulled Him aside for some one-on-one time.

"Then Peter took Him aside to speak to Him privately and began to reprove and charge Him sharply, saying, God forbid, Lord! This must never happen to You!" (Matthew 16:22 AMP).

When the Lord answered Peter in verse 23, it was not what he (Peter) was expecting, but the Lord knew whom He was actually speaking to. Peter may have had a revelation from God, but his soul realm (mind), was still under the influence of darkness. It was working overtime to try and rationalize what he heard. He had preset ideas and ways of doing things that were in his soul realm (mind) from his life before meeting Christ. Those preset tendencies went directly against the things of God.

The things of God cannot be rationalized with the soul (mind); they can only be revealed in spirit. Peter had a revelation. He knew a truth; he was actually speaking to the Truth, and wanted to see things worked out according to his own ways of seeing and doing things. He only saw as far as he could see in his own fleshly limitations. Peter received a revelation, but it came without an internal revolution. Maybe you find yourself as Peter did, trying to walk out a spiritual life based on soul realm training from a past life or fleshly skills and ability. This is a normal part of the journey. Overcoming this through submission to God as you hear from Holy Spirit is the solution.

You see Simon got alone with Christ one-on-one, and all his desires and thoughts were selfish; from a natural point of view. He was bending his knee but not breaking his "me." He had a revelation of Christ, but wanted to see Christ walk it out as he (Simon) saw fit.

He assumed that God's ways were the same as his ways; that God's thoughts were the same as his thoughts, that it would be Simon's "will" that would be done… He believed he had a better, wiser, easier way for the Lord to walk it all out. Oh, how many times I have come to God in prayer and told Him how I wanted things done? If not for His mercy and grace where would I be?

This was all done in the name of "looking out," in "love" and with the best of "*good* intentions." This friend is soul (mind) at its best, the know-it-all, and the rationalizer. The soul will use words strung together that sound like this: "If you are a real friend…" "If you really love him/her…" "If you were the one who really wanted to …" fill in the blanks. This is all a soul realm ploy to get me to act OUTSIDE of the guidance and will of Holy Spirit. Leaning on my own understanding outside of Christ is detrimental to my relationship with God as Father. Anything we do that is not originating from Holy Spirit comes from one other place, my soul realm (mind/thoughts), and that has been preprogrammed by darkness. The programming has been going on for years through television, radio, music, commercials, movies, books, shows, school curriculums, and even some church traditions or poor teachings.

I may have a revelation of who Christ is, but will remain infantile and fruitless, unless I am habitually putting to death the works of the flesh through obedience to Holy Spirit. I will have a form of godliness but deny the power thereof. I speak of MYSELF and the hundreds if not thousands upon thousands of times; I came to the Lord and had not bent my "me." Obviously, I will have struggles with flesh and soul as long as I am in this un-regenerated earth-suit. I know this. It does, however, become easier to spot as I mature spiritually and learn to listen to Holy Spirit, and allow His Truth to re-write my old understanding of things.

My first step toward victory was to take a look at my walk and ask Holy Spirit to guide me into all Truth. I began by answering these questions regarding yielding: *"When I bend my knee am I bending my me?"* Am I putting the Lord's will first? Am I allowing Him to tell me what to do? And am I willing to walk out HIS plan for my life, as opposed to my own?

THIS is where my soul realm (my mind) kicks in. You see; I was raised by the world and its way of doing things.

"For the god of this world has blinded the unbelievers' minds [that they should not discern the truth], preventing them from seeing the illuminating light of the Gospel of the glory of Christ (the Messiah), Who is the Image *and* Likeness of God" (2 Corinthians 4:4 AMP).

The type of music I listened to, what I watched on television, what books I read, how I was raised, whom I interacted with, all of this had a major role in how I saw things in the natural/carnal world. It had formed opinions in the old me and had given the old me an identity. Sadly, these were all planted in my soul (mind) and had me focused on my flesh (earth-suit) rather than on whom I am; spirit. This focus keeps me from knowing who He is in me…the Christ.

Dealing with my soul–realm is my biggest battle. The majority of what I learned in the world (even the best of it) is offensive to God when I try to live by it rather than allowing myself to be led by Holy Spirit. I needed to get on a detoxification program. Detox from what? My own un-regenerated mind; "[That is] because the mind of the flesh [with its carnal thoughts and purposes] is hostile to God, for it does not submit itself to God's Law; indeed it cannot" (Romans 8:7 AMP).

Like my Mom would say; I was infected with concepts, precepts, doctrines and demonization's that kept me from flowing correctly in spirit and they all resided in my soul (mind). If my own thoughts are not to be trusted; then HOW does one get the mind of Christ? How do I walk one on one with the Lord? How can I overcome these old ideas and attitudes?

For in one avenue of thought I may look good to the world, but in the other, I look like my Father's intent for Adam, to be Christ-like here on earth.

Part Two

Coming into an understanding

As I entered the restroom; I felt badly about something I had done. I randomly picked up several comic books off the racks as I walked by so I could have some reading material as I attended to my body's urgent need. There was a sign on the restroom door that read "No unpaid merchandise beyond this point." I knew it was wrong; however the thought of turning around to put them back was not being entertained.

I sat down in the stall, thanking God that I had not had an accident on the way to the restroom. I began to read my first comic book. Half-way through, it dawned on me; I was not having a bowel movement. Nothing, nada, zilch, not even gas. What was going on? I finished reading the comic book and felt kind of silly just sitting on a public restroom toilet without anything to do. So I quickly got up, washed my hands and exited the restroom. I thought if I could find a chair outside of the restroom by the reading area; I could wait this out and not have another urge to "go" in the car.

I thought I knew what was going on, but I didn't have a clue.

Chapter 5

D.N.A vs. G.N.A

"I do not understand what I do. For what I want to do I do not do, but what I hate I do" (Romans 7:15 NIV).

What interferes with the bending of my "me?" What hinders my growth in spirit? As I asked these questions, Holy Spirit made it clear in prayer. I had been introduced to a worldly meme disguised as a Kingdom Principal, infected with a religious virus and interrupted in my maturing as spirit. This was accomplished with a Belief System (B.S.) that did not apply to me. I was born again, but still living my life in the natural. I had a "form" of godliness but denied the power thereof. I was still following my soul realm; I still had opinions, ideas and thoughts I swore were correct. I was born-again, but I had a former life I had to keep forgetting and a new life I needed to be guided in. What a mess.

The B.S. (Belief System) religion gave me was that I could do things, and be part of "things" like groups and studies to become more like God, and in this B.S. I was substituting relationship with Holy Spirit for activities and a soul-realm education of who man told me God was. My first step was to understand and realize that, as a spirit being, I had to learn to listen to Holy Spirit. This is only done in spirit. After all, I was promised that He (Holy Spirit) will guide me.

"But when He, the Spirit of Truth (the Truth-giving Spirit) comes, He will guide you into all the Truth (the whole, full Truth). For He will not speak His own message [on His own authority]; but He will tell whatever He hears [from the Father; He will give the message that has been given to Him], and He will announce *and* declare to you the things that are to come [that will happen in the future]" (John 16:13 AMP).

Now this is a promise the Lord gave to all those that are born again in Him. So what hinders this? What gets in my way from experiencing a relationship with God in spirit?

My own D.N.A. is my enemy. In my walk, I have an inner thought process to deal with. I have to look at myself in the mirror and deal with my body and how it looks. Maybe I see myself as overweight, or not big enough. Maybe my hair is too long, or I need more hair, or it is too curly, and I need to have "good hair." Maybe my hair is too straight and needs some "life and bounce" to it. Maybe I think a new car will "show" how God has blessed me. Get it? How much of my focus is on identity and how I look in the flesh?

Personally, I had to deal with what I thought were racial issues. My earth-suit (body/flesh) looks a certain way, and I was told that others with different skin tones did not see me in a good light. This was the fascination the world had infected me with. I was told I had to live up to the history my "ancestors" had. I was encouraged to study it to know who I was. I was focused on my flesh. As I came to understand this walk in Christ and to see myself as a born-again being and as I focused on Him and not on the lies the world had impregnated my mind with, I tasted freedom. I realized there were only two races on the earth according to God, saved and unsaved. Everything else is a moot point. Everything else is a distraction from whom He wants me to be.

This was not an overnight change. It took a lot of "me" bending, and time with Holy Spirit to embrace truth and step away from the lie. My soul-realm (my mind) made sure on a daily basis that I was reminded of my abilities in the flesh. It was D.N.A. focused. I came into the body of Christ, born again in spirit, yet, I was trying to walk it out in the flesh, based on what I learned BEFORE my new birth; the Belief System (B.S.) religion was trying to poison me with.

D.N.A. = Devil Needs Attention

Devil Needs Attention that is what D.N.A means for a Christian. My focus on the flesh for identity, or on any of its attributes, for reliance without Christ is detrimental to my growth in knowing whom I am (a spirit-man), who He is in me (the Christ) and what He desires most (true relationship). This old nature keeps my "growing into Christ-likeness" stunted. Anytime I am thinking about myself and "me," I am focused on my D.N.A. which includes:

- What I may need
- What I may want
- What I think is going to happen
- Identity in the flesh
- Dependence on self

The devil wants me to be in *his* realm; the fear-realm, the self-realm, and the soul-realm he tainted. Just as God works through Faith and Favor, darkness works through fear and falsehoods. Just as God wants me to grow into His son, darkness wants me to stay spiritually retarded. Darkness attacks me in my soul-realm, with ideas and memories of a past life. My Father wants me to trust in Him and move in Spirit, and in faith, into the future He has written. Darkness reminds me of someone else's past, a dead man's past. That is not my past because that person has passed away. Holy Spirit reminds me of who I am in Him and whom I am meant to look like NOW as He leads me daily until the Lord returns and I get my glorified body and transformed mind.

All those thoughts that are not of my Father are to be cast down and brought into submission to the Truth of Christ. Those thoughts and ideas are from a past that does not belong to me; the same past that tries to fuel fear and doubt which is against what the Lord says I am to focus on. I refuse to focus on my flesh or be anxious, that is a soul-realm illusion. I am spirit. I will not look in the mirror and make that my identity. My standard is Christ and Christ alone.

"Therefore do not worry *and* be anxious, saying, what are we going to have to eat? or, What are we going to have to drink? or, What are we going to have to wear? For the Gentiles (heathen) wish for *and* crave *and* diligently seek all these things, and your heavenly Father knows well that you need them all. But seek (aim at and strive after) first of all His kingdom and His righteousness **[His way of doing and being right],** and then all these things taken together will be given you besides" (Matthew 6:31-33 AMP, emphasized words added).

I know my soul-realm (my mind) will try to drive me to be fearful. My soul-realm (mind) asks: "How will I pay my bills? What will I eat? How will I get things done? When will I get married? Will I die alone and old?" "Will I have a child?" These concerns are all based on what I have learned, heard, or believed in the past. These were thoughts the former me had entertained. He has died; he has passed away. I, the one writing this book, am a brand new creature. A new creation; birthed to mature and grow to look like my heavenly Father. My example of this Lifestyle is Christ Jesus.

Darkness wants me to move in the natural as I focus on my own abilities and an identity outside of Christ. My Father, on the other hand, does not want me to live in that illusion. He wants me to live in Reality, the *super*-natural. He desires that I seek Him, get closer to Him, be intimate with Him and listen to what Holy Spirit shares with me as I pray and seek more of His presence and power in my life.

Am I truly listening all the time? And if not; what has my attention other than Him?

My former self (not born-again) had a lot of strongholds of past hurts, and fears in my soul (mind). My Father has a Garden of Eden type of life for me. He has a plan where I am at rest waiting for His next move in and through me as I mature in Christ. My garden, unfortunately, was in need of attention. The flower beds of Love, Joy, and Peace were not blossoming because they were covered with weeds. These weeds came from what I once innocently allowed darkness to plant in me through others as they shared their own views based on <u>their own</u> hurts, fears and belief system. These weeds were realities outside of Christ I stepped into willingly. I have two characters in me competing for control: my soul (thoughts, emotions, ideas, and opinions *without* Holy Spirit) and my spirit, as guided by Holy Spirit. And BOTH soul and spirit are manifested externally through the body. I had to pick a side.

Take a look at how it is described in Romans 8 in the Amplified Bible.

"For those who are according to the flesh *and* are controlled by its unholy **desires** set their **minds** on *and* pursue those things which **gratify the flesh**, but those who are according to the Spirit *and* are <u>**controlled by the desires of the Spirit set their minds on and seek those things which gratify the [Holy] Spirit.**</u> Now the *mind of the flesh* **[which is sense and reason without the Holy Spirit]** is death [death that comprises all the miseries arising from sin, **both here and hereafter**]. But the mind of the [Holy] <u>***Spirit is life*** **and [soul] peace [both now and foreve**</u>r]. [That is] because the mind of the flesh [with its *carnal thoughts and purposes*] **is hostile**

to God, for it does not submit itself to God's Law; indeed it cannot. So then those who are living the life of the flesh [catering to the appetites and impulses of their carnal nature] **cannot please** *or* **satisfy God,** *or* **be acceptable to Him**" (Romans 8:5-8 AMP, emphasis added).

So my carnal-nature, my thoughts and self-serving ways are against God and only serve one purpose; to give the devil the attention he so craves.

"Now the doings (practices) of the flesh are clear (obvious): they are immorality, impurity, indecency, Idolatry, sorcery, enmity, strife, jealousy, anger (ill temper), selfishness, divisions (dissensions), party spirit (factions, sects with peculiar opinions, heresies), Envy, drunkenness, carousing, and the like…" (Galatians 5:19-21 AMP).

My ability to know what each one of these words means and recognize these things working in ME is paramount to my relationship with God as Father and my maturing. Coming to recognize these works in myself is of greater urgency than me seeing or discerning them in anyone else. It is only by my being transparent with God and then asking Holy Spirit to reveal my works of the flesh that I can grow. As I listen to Holy Spirit and turn away from my D.N.A., I start to embrace my G.N.A. It is in this embracing, in this purposeful choice, in this one decision to listen to Holy Spirit and grow in my G.N.A. that I can begin to see God's original intent for Adam, and now for myself.

G.N.A. = God's New Attributes

God's New Attributes is where I have decided to focus my attention on. It is in the newness of His Life in me that I can say I have enjoyment. This, however, takes an understanding that I cannot accomplish any growth under my own power or will.

The Word of God states the following: "But you are **not** living the life of the flesh, you **are living** the **life** of the **Spirit**, if the [Holy] Spirit of God [really] dwells within you [directs and controls you]. But if anyone does not possess the [Holy] Spirit of Christ, he is none of His [he does not belong to Christ, is not truly a child of God]" (Romans 8:9 AMP, emphasis added).

I find I have never walked like this before. There is nothing in my mental library or earthly experiences that can or could prepare me for this new spiritual lifestyle. I need someone that has done this before, a Teacher was needed; a Guide.

For example: When I moved into my first home, I needed a guide, someone that had done things around a home before. I found an awesome handyman. He proved to be a guide, a helper, and in certain instances, a comforter. I also required the services of a grounds keeper, a plumber, and a pool boy who taught me what I needed to know about taking care of my new home. I slowly became adept at taking care of most minor home issues and a few major. When I became a broker, I needed a mentor, someone to guide me, to teach me how to write deals, to lead me on an honest path and assist me in applying what I had learned. My mentor "showed me the ropes" and let me slowly grow into being a master broker.

Similarly, I had never been born-again. This is a brand new life, a spiritual walk, new to me. And God sent me a guide, Holy Spirit. He reveals more and more of the real-me daily. He shares with me daily what He wants me to do, where He wants me to go, and what, if anything, He wants me to say. Granted I have spiritual parents that have helped me along the way, but they only focus on building up the Christ in me. They continuously point me to Christ and reinforce my need for prayer, intimacy and correctly hearing as I practice standing still. They lovingly remind me that it is in my willingness to His obedience that I can eat the good of the land. With great patience, they pray, cover and bless me as the Lord leads. They help speed up my growth by their consistent Christ-like lifestyle and ability to stay out of God's way as He works with me. Therefore, I have to know my Father's voice so I can recognize it as it comes through Holy Spirit as I pray and other means that He chooses. As I recognize His voice I have to be teachable, trainable and humble to be taught by Christ through them, but they are never the substitute for a relationship with God as Father.

Unfortunately, my soul-realm (mind) has its own ideas. My flesh has its own desires, and passions and that can hinder my walk as a spiritual being. Remember when I discussed the *scuba suit*, and *space suit*? Have you ever watched someone walking under water or on the moon; maybe in a movie? They move around with their bulky suit in a kind of robotic way. They do not have the "freedom of flow" as when they have the suit off. Do you agree? Well in this earth-suit (flesh) I have sin, and in my un-renewed soul (mind) I have the old training of this world, and both the traditions of flesh and prior training of my soul (mind) weigh me down, and do not allow me to have the "freedom of flow" as when I am with my Father walking in and as spirit. That is why we have that constant battle within ourselves and why spiritual maturity is needed.

I am still growing and not matured yet, but as I grow daily into His likeness by listening and willingly obeying I do have progress. As I grow in love with Him, He reveals more of Himself to me. It is in this walk that I find my purpose. So what does this maturity look like in Spirit? What would be the indicators for maturity? Good question. Here is a God answer:

"But the fruit of the [Holy] Spirit [**the work which His presence within accomplishes**] is love, joy (gladness), peace, patience (an even temper, forbearance), kindness, goodness (benevolence), faithfulness, Gentleness (meekness, humility), self-control (self-restraint, continence). Against such things there is no law [that can bring a charge]. And those who belong to Christ Jesus (the Messiah) have crucified the flesh (the godless human nature) with its passions and appetites *and* desires. If we live by the [Holy] Spirit, let us also walk by the Spirit. [If by the Holy Spirit we have our life in God, let us go forward walking in line, our conduct controlled by the Spirit.]" (Galatians 5:22-25 AMP, emphasis added).

My G.N.A *(God's New Attributes)* is manifested in the Fruit of the Spirit. They start with Love, (Agape), the God kind of Love, the unconditional Love. The kind of Love that in soul-realm (my mind) and flesh (my body) is impossible to manifest. The kind of Love that does not see color of skin, type of culture, language spoken or even scorn by loved ones. The kind of Love that is not influenced by past hurts (whether fifty years ago or five minutes ago) by people of a different look, political affiliation or gender issues. This Love is not based on quid pro quo or based on a sex life. This love is not based on what "the world says" or on how "I was raised." This is a Love that can only be matured, manifested, and experienced in spirit. This comes through a relationship with Holy Spirit. It cannot be learned. **It has to be revealed**. God is Spirit. Therefore, His new attributes in me, this fruit, are also in spirit. The external demonstration of this fruit in my walk is proof of Who is growing inside of me.

As we go down the list, each fruit gives birth to the next one. Love, brings me joy which is my strength, and that gives me peace, allowing me to have patience (an even temper, forbearance) so that I can be full of kindness, and goodness (benevolence), with faithfulness to my Father. Showing gentleness (meekness, humility), and self-control through Christ in my decisions and not being abrupt or moving off of soul and flesh. G.N.A. focus can only be done in Christ and allows me to be led by Holy Spirit so I can grow into what Adam was made for, to be a son. My example of this is Jesus Christ.

A deliberate move on my part to "***be still*** and know" He is God (Psalm 46:10 NKJV, emphasis added) is mandatory. I need to have faith, not just in the Bible, but in what I hear from Him on a <u>*daily basis*</u> in my prayer closet. Worship/relationship with God is a spirit thing meaning a transparent and truthful thing.

Soul (my mind) and flesh (my body) have nothing to do with my spiritual walk. Staying in His Grace and dealing with these obstacles by His power is the only way to get them both out of His way. I said, "His way" because as I submit to Him He can have His way in and through me. I can walk in my purpose. When I let my guard down as I follow thoughts and fears from the past that do not belong to me I am sure of becoming one who is focused on the bending of my knee, rather than the breaking of my "me." The bending of my knee outwardly looks good and can sometimes be influenced by my need to look a certain way.

The bending of my "me" is an internal voluntary action in His power by His grace because I experienced His Love. That's God!

Chapter 6

Growing in Him

"When I was a boy of 14, my father was so ignorant I could hardly stand to have the old man around. But when I got to be 21, I was astonished at how much the old man had learned in seven years." Mark Twain

Here is a question for you: How did Christ make it from the baptism to the cross? The answer is; "By following Holy Spirit."

John 5:19 and 5:30 are two of those scriptures that just humble and challenge me every time I read them. Christ Himself waited to be guided every step of the way. He waited to hear and then He obeyed. Even His teachings according to John 5:17 were shared with Him from His Father. These verses started me on a path of introspection. I asked the Lord: "What am I doing? I mean yes, I can read the Bible, and yes I can preach, but so can millions of people. What is different about me? Am I listening to you Lord? Am I giving YOUR message at the appointed time or am I just going off of MY own talents and gifts?" Who was I really serving?

One day, in prayer, I asked the Lord to show me what He wanted me to pull back from, and to my soul's unbelief, He wanted me out of that church flow. He wanted me to stop all the extra-curricular activities and get down to the meat and potatoes of Loving Him, to be focused on Him, to grow in Him. He told me He had a message for me to share and I needed to be still. That the entire "ministry" thing was just getting in the way. I was so concerned with looking good, by "doing" things and "attending" things that I was not spending the time HE wanted me to spend with Him. Not the amount of time *I thought* was sufficient, but the time HE desired I spend with Him.

This was hard for me to swallow because I had my identity in ministry; I had all my friends in ministry, and I was being told I would be a pastor the following year at a popular local church. How could I leave that? The answer was easy; the execution was difficult.

It became clear that darkness had come to me in a subtle manner. The devil had replaced my love for looking good in the world with my love to look good by serving in the church. Both were leading me away from relationship with God. I turned away from the funnel of death and spent time talking to my Father. One on one, listening and learning, first fifteen minutes, then thirty, later came an hour, then hours, and it grew from there. Prayer is an overflow of relationship with God, and the more I knew Him as Father, and then Daddy, the closer we became. Regular prayer was a starting point; intimate relationship was the goal, and constant prayer was a side effect.

This led me to grow in Christ, slowly maturing at times, and at times it seemed like overnight I was "adjusted" in my thinking; and I was being transformed. Then there are days I feel like I have not matured enough, and on these days He reminds me that His Grace is sufficient. Slowly, His thoughts were becoming my thoughts; I was doing things His way and finding my peace and joy in it. I have yet to reach any level of greatness, but I press on to that goal that I desire more than anything; Christ-likeness. I desire relationship with God as my Abba, my Dad.

As I prayed and spent time with Holy Spirit, I started to ask Him questions that I had pondered. He answered me, and the answers had me in awe. One of the main things I learned is that there is a time frame when all born-again believers seem to be just like the world. This is because they are still babies, unable to talk Kingdom language and unable to manifest Him yet. THIS is where darkness wants to keep us as a Body, retarded; still on milk, babies. Now some may have an instant change, but I've never met those. All the saints I know that have matured a great deal all did it over time, and they all struggled with issues.

Paul planted a church where he began teaching and guiding them until they were able to hear from and talk to God on their own; then he left. Later on Paul wrote back regarding some questions this particular church had and some things he had heard. He was not exactly pleased with their lack of maturing. He obviously had a time frame in mind that was acceptable to still be immature. The time frame seems to have passed, and he wrote:

"HOWEVER, BRETHREN, I could not talk to you as to

spiritual [men], but as to nonspiritual [men of the flesh, in whom the carnal nature predominates], as to mere infants [in the new life] in Christ [unable to talk yet!]… For you are still [unspiritual, having the nature] of the flesh [under the control of ordinary impulses]. For as long as [there are] envying and jealousy *and* wrangling and factions among you, are you not unspiritual *and* of the flesh, behaving yourselves after a human standard *and* like mere (unchanged) men?" (1 Corinthians 3:1 and 3 AMP, emphasis added).

Paul already knew the truth. Once they were born again they had a new nature and a new character. (2 Corinthians 5:17). However, these believers were not walking this out and waiting on the Lord; they were focused on other things, not of God and distracted with their old natures' views and thoughts. They were immature and still sounding, looking and acting like the world. They did not continue to pursue that relationship with the Lord. They became slow to hear and quick to act it seems.

Speaking to believers in the book of Hebrews, Holy Spirit says to that church: "Concerning this we have much to say which is hard to explain, since you have become dull in your [spiritual] hearing *and* sluggish [even slothful in achieving spiritual insight]" (Hebrews 5:11 AMP). Did you get that? They wanted to share deeper revelations with them but could not because they had become sluggish in their spiritual hearing. That's where the modern church is today. Most teaching has not incorporated that we are spirit and then expounding on Kingdom principles because many are teaching flesh based messages. We have tried to walk this out in everything but spirit, and that has failed horribly. The new nature is the only thing that matters or is of any importance. Paul understood that to walk this walk; he needed to put to death that body of sin he was carrying around with him on a daily basis. He understood that this was going to take renewing of the mind, putting aside his own upbringing and former beliefs. This was such an urgent matter to him that he stopped his scribe who was writing to the church at Galatia, and he, himself took up the quill and parchment and began to write (never seen of Paul before in the New Testament).

"See with what large letters I am writing with my own hand. [Mark carefully these closing words of mine]" (Galatians 6:11 AMP).

What was it? What was His great message? What was so important to convey?

"For neither is circumcision [now] of any importance, nor un-circumcision, **but [only] a new creation [the result of a new birth and a new nature in Christ Jesus, the Messiah]**" (Galatians 6:15 AMP, emphasis added).

We should not depend on what was in the past or our flesh, period. The only thing that matters in the pursuit of God; in the growing into Christ-likeness is the new birth and THE NEW NATURE!

Yes, there is a time period where we should expect ourselves and others who are newly born-again to still resemble the world. After all this is not an overnight thing. Peter, Paul, and Thomas, as a matter of fact ALL of the Apostles, had periods displaying a predominance of immaturity, lack of growth and carnal-nature. The enemy wants to keep us spiritually retarded, not growing, totally stuck in pre-school. My responsibility is to notice these things in me as Holy Spirit reveals them and to turn from darkness to light. I will never fully mature while wrapped in this body of death, however, I refuse to be found playing like a child in a sandbox when He returns.

Truthfully, I battle with my old nature daily. So did Paul. Apostle Paul said: "For I do not understand my own actions [I am baffled, bewildered]. I do not practice *or* accomplish what I wish, but I do the very thing that I loathe [which my moral instinct condemns]" (Romans 7:15 AMP).

Yes, this walk was going to take maturity and growth in spirit; the kind you can only get through experiencing Christ. The only one to train me is Holy Spirit. I may have a Teacher, Pastor, Evangelist, Prophet or Apostle sharing THEIR experiences and revelations, but I needed to get my own. Seriously, how can I eat and be full when someone else is doing the chewing and swallowing? Many go to Sunday service and listen to man but possibly have never really had a True and intimate relationship with God as Father. Much less Abba, Daddy. They suffer from second-hand religion, and hand-me-down revelations.

So how do I step into this new life? Well Christ made a statement that is quite revelatory once you understand it. "Jesus said to him, I am the Way and the Truth and the Life; no one comes to the Father except by (through) Me" (John 14:6 AMP).

We need to understand WHAT Life Christ spoke of. In the same way, we needed to be clear on the words: Create, make and form. We also need to be clear on the three words in Greek used for life. For in understanding this, we will have a clearer picture of what the Lord was, and still is saying to us.

In the New Testament, we find the following Greek words for life: Zoë, psyche, and bios. Each one individually can be translated as "life," but they provide three pivotal distinctions in the Christian walk.

Bios: The world of the flesh

The life, with which I deal with, interact with and see people in, is bios (Strong's Greek Concordance #979).

The word biology is derived from the word bios. Biology is a natural science with the study of the body and life of living organisms. This is the way the majority of the world views life and many Christians are finding themselves trying to compete with this measuring stick. They live in a bios world and use the so-called "success" in this world to judge an internal relationship with God. This life, however, is the least important in the New Testament. Bios always refers to life as quantity; what I earn, own or can do. It is also the most readily available life to discuss since it can be measured by what we see. Statements are made like: I own a house; I have two cars, and I just purchased a new set of golf clubs. I have _____ (fill in the blank). You get the picture. Now there is NOTHING wrong with being blessed IF and when it comes from the Lord. I have no qualms or disagreement with Christians being well off, out of debt and living well. I am just sharing how bios life is experienced. The bios life is viewed in appearances and in the manifestations of things. It is a surface life, and can never be a determination of spiritual maturity or necessarily people being "blessed." From Matthew to Revelation this noun appears ten times.

It is used for a somewhat neutral designation of wealth and health or the lack thereof. The poor widow in Mark 12:44, who cast her two lepta into the temple treasury, threw in her "whole life."

"For all *they* did cast in of their abundance; but she of her want did cast in all that she had, *even* all her living [bios]." (Mark 12:44 KJV, "bios" added).

The woman with the issue of blood who touched the Lord's finished garment (the hem) in Luke 8:43 is described as having exhausted her "whole life" on physicians.

"And a woman having an issue of blood twelve years, which had spent all her living [**bios**] upon physicians, neither could be healed of any" (Luke 8:43 KJV, "bios" added).

What of the story of the prodigal son? The father divided his "life" with his sons (Luke 15:12).

"And the younger of them said to his father, Father, give me the portion of goods that falleth to me. And he divided unto them his living [**bios**]" (Luke 15:12 KJV, "bios" added).

Whoever has the life of the world, we read in 1 John 3:17, and hardens his heart in the face of the need of his brothers cannot say he has the love of God.

"But whoso hath this world's good [**bios**], and seeth his brother have need, and shutteth up his bowels of compassion from him, how dwelleth the love of God in him?" (1 John 3:17 KJV, "bios" added).

I will break down the last verse by using more explanatory translations of the Greek as it is expressed in the Amplified Bible and The Living Bible translations of the same verse.

"But if anyone has this world's goods (resources for sustaining life) and sees his brother *and* fellow believer in need, yet closes his heart of compassion against him, how can the love of God live *and* remain in him?" (1 John 3:17 AMP).

"But if someone who is supposed to be a Christian has money enough to live well, and sees a brother in need, and won't help him—how can God's love be within *him?*" (1 John 3:17 TLB).

Bios is based on the flesh and "its" abilities and outward appearances. In this, we find physical health and wealth, in this we interact with others. Here, we also get attacked by sickness, dis-ease, and needs. The New Testament does not consider this living. These things are just the manifestations of the world, and my individual efforts in it. Real life? Well, that comes from His Reality.

Psyche: The world of the mind

The second word that can be used for life is psyche (Strong's Greek Concordance #5590). Living in the psyche (soul-realm) is as dangerous for a Christian as bios. As I shared before, this is the word we use to form the words psychology and psychiatry, also known as the study and the healing of the mind. The ratio is almost ten to one between psyche and bios. Psyche may be mentioned more because it gives the impression of the character of life as opposed to just a physical description.

For example, if a friend were describing someone to you as "tall, attractive, physically fit, awesome eyes, well-dressed with expensive taste in jewelry he/she wears," that would be bios. If they then said, "He is racist, makes fun of people, is a liberal, is scared of spiders and loves to discuss their love of modern art"...well, that is psyche. Soul realm, their mind, thoughts and ideas etc.

Psyche is your feelings emotions and will; your quick wit, your ability to think, your goal setting, your beliefs, attitudes and fears. This would be your personality. Jesus Christ said: "Therefore I say unto you, Take no thought for your life [psyche], what ye shall eat, or what ye shall drink; nor yet for your body, what ye shall put on. Is not the life [psyche] more than meat, and the body than raiment?" (Matthew 6:25 KJV, "psyche" added).

"Therefore I tell you, stop being perpetually uneasy (anxious and worried) about your life, what you shall eat *or what you shall drink;* or about your body, what you shall put on. Is not life greater [in quality] than food, and the body [far above and more excellent] than clothing?" (Matthew 6:25 AMP).

The Lord warned us about psyche life in the scriptures. We should not be anxious, or worry about what we will eat, drink or wear. For these things are concerns of those that HAVE NO GOD.

"Therefore do not worry *and* be anxious, saying, What are we going to have to eat? or, What are we going to have to drink? or, What are we going to have to wear? For the Gentiles (heathen) wish for *and* crave *and* diligently seek all these things, and your heavenly Father knows well that you need them all" (Matthew 6:31-32 AMP).

Anxious is defined as "worried and tense because of possible misfortune, danger, etc; uneasy" (Collins English Dictionary). This describes a state of mind which can lead to a poor state of bios (body) due to the ramifications of stress, worrying, and concern. This is a life with no peace and it will drain the body. I have faced weight gain, lack of sleep and adrenal fatigue to a point that I was unable to function properly in my day-to-day lifestyle. Then I stepped into His Reality and found peace and healing. That is why He gave us instructions for our soul-realm. "But seek (aim at and strive after) first of all His kingdom and His righteousness (His way of doing and being right), and then all these things taken together will be given you besides" (Matthew 6:33 AMP).

This involves me changing the way I think. This involves me **learning**, **leaning on**, and **living out** the promises of God. Building a relationship with Him and hearing, not just the written word (it can start there), but also the spoken Word is paramount. The world will try to get me to conform to its ways of doing things, to its beliefs of living in self, having dependency on what I have read, watched or believe to be true. I was trained to see education as the end-all, and to my own thoughts, as the cure-all. Christians, on the other hand, have been given instructions to do the following:

"Do not be conformed to this world (this age), [fashioned after and adapted to its external, superficial customs], but be transformed (changed) by the [entire] renewal of <u>**your mind**</u> [**by its new ideals and its new attitude**], so that you may prove [for yourselves] what is the good and acceptable and perfect will of God, *even* the thing which is good and acceptable and perfect [in **His sight for you**]" (Romans 12:2 AMP, emphasis added).

The battlefield is in the un-renewed mind. My new birth was in spirit and not in soul. When He comes back, my glorified body will have a transformed soul. For now, I listen to Him and allow His thoughts to become mine. I seek to be obedient, so His ways become my ways and God can then manifest His Love through me.

Some Christians are still stuck on bios. Focusing on what they have or on what they feel the Lord blessed them with; in other words, what they may have acquired without God. Others are stuck on psyche; what they think they learned, read, or heard before the new birth; in other words, their beliefs outside of God.

While bios represents external efforts and psyche reflects internal beliefs, both reflect a type of life, but neither one represents the Life Christ said He came to give more abundantly. The life that is in God stems from God and IS God!

Zoë: The God Life

Zoë is one word for the born-again believer that takes precedence over all three Greek words for "life." Zoë defines the Life that is God's Life. When we are born again, we are translated from a dead spirit (without God), to a living being, infused with Holy Spirit and full of Life! It is the most vital of the three words and understanding it is paramount to a Christian's walk. While man can plant a seed and have a tree grow, or impregnate a woman who gives birth to a baby; that serves to illustrate bios life (flesh). If I implant an idea, start a belief and teach a culture, this is an example of psyche (soul-realm) life. Zoë, on the other hand, comes from God alone. "Whatever is born of flesh [bios] is flesh [bios]. Whatever is born of Spirit [meaning Holy Spirit] is spirit" (John 3:6 NKJV, "bios" added).

"What is born of [from] the flesh is flesh [of the physical is physical]; and what is born of the Spirit is spirit" (John 3:6 AMP).

How do we get life? "It is the **Spirit Who gives life** [He is the Life-giver]; the **flesh conveys no benefit whatever** [there is no profit in it]. The words (truths) that I have been speaking to you are spirit and life [Zoë]" (John 6:63 AMP, "Zoë" and emphasis added).

Bios defines where I find my D.N.A, but Zoë is where my G.N.A exists and flows from. My psyche or soul realm needs to be controlled by me as spirit. This can only happen as I am guided by Holy Spirit. Then and only then can my bios life manifest outwardly the Zoë life that is in me. Get it?

God is never referred to as bios or psyche. Whenever we read of the God kind of Life, it means Zoë. Prior to my rebirth, I had bios life obviously, and I had psyche life, but Zoë only came when I was born-again; and that was a gift. I did nothing to deserve earn or expect it. It was pure favor based on my acknowledging my position at that moment as a sinner and my need for Jesus Christ as my savior and Lord of all.

Minister Dale Fletcher, M.S., founder of Faith and Health Connection, a non-profit organization in North Carolina, was kind enough to bless us with the following graphic. We are a three part whole moving as one, but only one part was created to have control; the spirit.

This is an example of how we are designed to function with the emphasis that in me (spirit) is where Holy Spirit makes His residence in us. In spirit is where we hear and receive revelations as well as build relationship with God.

You ARE represented by that middle circle, spirit, the true you. The surrounding circles represent the suit you are dressed in. Focus on the love, purpose and meaning of God in YOU as spirit and I can guarantee that all false realities will fall away.

We Are a 3-Part Whole

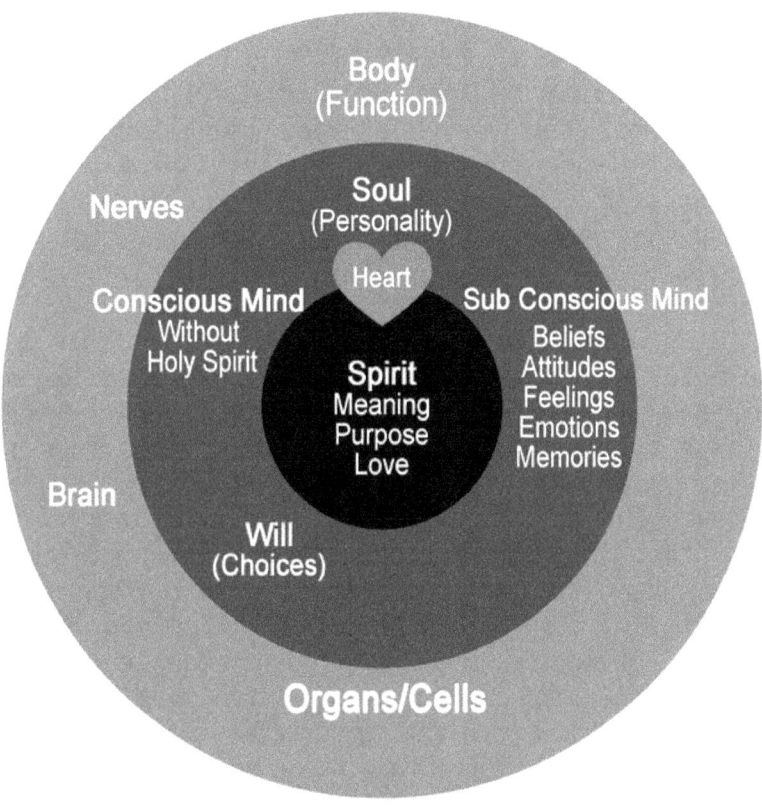

We are spirit, have a soul and live in a body

It is very possible to live and die only experiencing bios and psyche, for those who never received the God life through Jesus Christ. Sadly, for a born-again believer it is also possible to be retarded spiritually due to poor teaching, disobedience or a mixture of both, and never experience the Zoë life of God.

Let me be clear that the gifts and callings of God are without repentance. My abilities in bios, and attributes in psyche are God given. What I had to come to accept is that my gifts and abilities do not bring me closer into a relationship with God. All my gifting and abilities put together in my pocket with a five dollar bill will only afford me a medium sized caramel latte at my local fancy coffee shop. Without the character of Christ, my gifting is useless, self-serving and at best deceptive. When God made the earth-suit for Adam, God formed the bios from the dust of the earth; He then breathed into the nostrils the Life breath, or the Zoë of man, and that union created a living psyche. Now this comes only through revelation. Many may read this and still be void of any understanding what this means exactly. Others may have a certain "degree" of understanding. God loves you where you are and will meet you right there.

As you read and then re-read this book and walk out your Zoë (Life) in Him, you will get a deeper understanding as you experience His Word and revelations in a more tangible way. I wish there was a shortcut, but it starts at the bending of your "me" through dedicated quantity of quality prayer and alone time and ends with the building of Him in you. That beloved is a lifetime journey.

Time is the enemy of bios, and complacency is the trap of psyche, but Zoë has only one enemy; sin. Satan intends for me to stay as a Zoë baby; without experiences, underfed, anemic and lethargic. You see, if he cannot stop me from being born-again, then his intentions are that I stay in an infantile stage, suckling on milk, focused on bios and psyche rather than Zoë. The focus of the first two are knowledge, Bible memorization and service to the church etc.; it looks so good, feels good and is acknowledged by others as good.

Living a Zoë lifestyle requires standing still. It requires being focused on listening, and as I hear, going out willingly and obeying. It is a process that normally involves doing the very opposite of what my flesh feels like doing and what my soul thinks is best. Zoë is a real Life. After all, Jesus Christ Himself said: "The thief comes only in order to steal and kill and destroy. **I came that they may have *and* enjoy life [Zoë], and have it in abundance (to the full, till it overflows)**" (John 10:10 AMP, "Zoë" and emphasis added).

If I only focus on prospering in Bios, and psyche lifestyles, it will keep my real Life from flowing. If I focus on prospering spiritually in Zoë life, then the life Christ came to give me will encompass all other manifestations of life. This can only be done as I build a relationship with God, and that is in experiential relationship, not an experimental one.

Chapter 7

Not all things are created equal

"What is your reality?" Derick Kuilan, bond-servant in the making.

I have had the honor to study with and have the Holy Spirit work through me to build up a young man named Derick Kuilan. When we first met, I saw a spark in Him that I recognized as Holy Spirit. I saw a hunger in him, not for knowledge, but, for relationship with God. I knew it was a God moment. Since we first met, he has grown by leaps and bounds in Holy Spirit, and although he may not appear to have reached any special level of greatness, I can say that he presses in to get more of Christ built up in him. It has positively affected his family, his leadership capabilities and his relationship with his wife. I can actually see his blessings and his desire to have more of Holy Spirit lead all avenues of his life. When I asked him how he became perceptive to Holy Spirit working in his life, this was his answer:

> *I started to notice I was not living in Reality. As a Christian, I was choosing to live in an illusion. Adding insult to injury, I was guarding that fake reality with a strong grip. As I spent time with my Father in prayer He taught me through you [Daniel], and in my alone time with Him; I started to look around me, at others in the Body and a question was birthed in me. I would ask them "What is your Reality?"*
>
> *The answers have varied. I realize that many have a focus on their earth-suit, race, and culture. While, for others, reality was their soul-realm, education, beliefs and what they had learned in seminary*

etc. I found this to be an issue both in and out of the church. While the world has a strong affiliation with self, I have found that, in the church, it is not much different. Many have a tendency to focus on information that they have learned, from man (a pastor, a teacher, parents or lifestyle). Still others believe that their titles (pastor, associate pastor, leader, officer, attorney etc.) are what qualify them to function in God's Kingdom. Granted they may possess a certain level of information and training in the natural realm, but in the supernatural realm they are only babies. Speaking of myself, I have a lot of room to grow still; just ask my wife.

Tapping into God's Reality is what has assisted my personal growth in the Lord. Yet at times I wonder how the modern church has been functioning without a True revelation of who they are. I found, in other places I studied at, that they based reality on self, what they have "done" and what they can "do", rather than on what Christ has done, which alone gains them access to Holy Spirit's leading and training. Many have yet to hear His voice, and those that do run off so quickly to brag about the first whisper, that they do not wait there patiently to hear more and fine-tune their listening.

Without true relation with Holy Spirit, they have blurred vision and at best are being led by some leader in the church or the latest popular book. Now I speak from personal experience and from personal failures. I had blurred vision even while in the church; I was leading a Bible study class and reading the Word daily, nonstop. Souls were being saved; folks wanted to get baptized, the Bible study was growing, people were learning and yet I had blurred vision. That blurred vision in that area of my life can all be summed up in one thing; lack of true relationship with God as Father.

When I started experiencing God speaking to me through Holy Spirit, and then began obeying what He said or asked me, to do, I found myself reaping the rewards of John 14:21, knowing Him more as He reveals Himself to me after I trust and rely on Him as He speaks. Once I stepped into the revelation that I am spirit, not a Hispanic or a white male, but spirit, my vision became clearer. Jesus said, "I am the Way, the Truth, and the Life" (John 14:6 NKJV, capitalization emphasis added). The same word, truth, in the Amplified Bible is translated as "reality" in John 4:24 and it is the same word used in John 4:23. Christ is the Reality; He is all, and in all, and anything outside of Him, ESPECIALLY for a Christian, is an illusion. When Jesus walked around on the earth and someone needed healing, He would tell them, "Your faith has made you well," meaning "healed you" (Luke 17:19 NKJV). Before coming to Him, they were in a "reality" not of Christ, one that said they were blind, sick, poor, unworthy, and dying, yet they made Him their Reality, and whether you were a scorned woman with an issue of blood or a mighty Centurion commander, your reality HAD TO become His and Him.

Once they replaced the illusion, they found themselves in and received the gift He was offering in His Reality, they stepped into THE Reality; the only one that matters. There was a shift from what they could do to what He could do. From earthly limitations to Heavenly limitless possibilities manifested through His Love and Grace. At the moment you receive this revelation of Reality, and to the degree you receive it and make it YOUR Reality, is to the degree that you will find the manifestation of the things you need to function here on earth.

Many Christians get sidetracked due to being "history majors." They are focused on ancient history, things of the past in their own lives. They focus on pains, hurts, and lies implanted in their soul realm by darkness working through friends, family, and circumstances. They lean on the education of their past and the relations they made. This hinders their growth and clouds their reality. They major on history rather than focusing on His-story. He came to set me free, and I am a brand new creation. As I walk from one experience to another experience in Him; I pass a few trials with flying colors, and others I do less than His best for me. In His

Reality, I can always get back up and start afresh with experience under my belt. That has become my Reality, and He has never let me down nor judged me for a failure. His is the only Reality I choose to guard today.

Now I wish I could take credit for what he had shared. I have been blessed to have the Lord work through me to teach him, and I am honored to have planted and watered. The deeper truths and the revelation given to Mr. Kuilan came as he prayed to His Father, and stayed still to listen to Holy Spirit. My prayer is that you will also read then re-read and pray about the Truths in this book and go to your Father and ask Him to make it increase in you; He will.

Mr. Kuilan prized what he had learned above all other things and then he walked them out. He is still walking them out, but he had a Christ experience and no one can tell him any different. This brings me to the next two words. Experience and Experiment. These two words are what make and break our walk. They sound alike, but they are light-years apart. Let me explain.

Experience or Experiment?

Experience. It is that one word we place so much value on. Are you hiring a lawyer? What experience does he/she have? Are you getting a plumber? Does he have experience? Whether a doctor or a surgeon; we want to know one thing. What is their experience like? Because we know the more someone does a certain action or works in a system, the better they are at it.

Experiment. Do you want a doctor to experiment on your child? On your spouse? On you? What if an attorney said they were going to "experiment" with a defense they never really used before, but had read about it? Worse case, you will get sentenced to life in prison. Would you be ok with that?

In my own walk, (or lack thereof) I found myself 100% experimenting with the Lord. I had a form of godliness, but I was denying the power thereof. I kept "reading" the Bible, going to church and reciting scripture. I became adept at this; I started to study, and I took up Greek and Hebrew, attended seminars and read books. All of this was nothing more than one great big experiment.

Reading the Bible has its place, but not over one on one

personal and intimate relationship with God as Father. After all, for many years there was no Bible put together, so dependence on HEARING from God for oneself was paramount. This was, and still is, accomplished the same way today, through Holy Spirit. Going to church has its place and is encouraged in scripture, but finding my identity in groups and classes is not what my Father has intended for me.

Imagine a parent that just had a baby. At the moment he/she is birthed the authorities come in, grab the child and take it away. It is raised with kindness; it is given a book about its parents; it is taught songs about them, and it even studies about them daily. Yes, the child speaks to them daily from a chair or in a room but never really hears the parents' voice continually. The child never hears the daily desires, and daily thoughts of its parents. The child never has an intimate personal relationship. The child shares with the parent by speaking into the air, or a pillow or while driving, about its needs and thoughts, fears and joys. Rarely if ever do they actually get back what their parent wants for that moment and they never actually get to distinguish the voice of their parent. What kind of relationship is that? Tell me, how could this child have a one-way relationship with that parent? The child is doing all that it thinks (soul realm) or has been taught or feels (flesh) is the best way to have a relationship except the way that the parent laid out. The parent wants to spend time with the child, one on one. Hours at a time loving the child and teaching it to be a re-presentation of the family he/she came from. The child focuses on "doing" things that seem to resemble what the parents want, but they can never be sure because they are not hearing daily from the parents. In this case, the child is a born-again believer; religion took them away from getting to know God as Father and taught them dependency on a building, a person, a group, a ministry, a doctrine…on everything, except God Himself.

That is what the many churches have done. Many have taken born-again believers and have kept them busy with all the "stuff" and "fluff" of the modern church times, but have not pointed them to the ministry that matters most. The ministry of knowing God rather than knowing "about" God.

I was experimenting with ways that I THOUGHT would help me to be godlier and more Christ-like. My soul realm had ideas that I learned in my past, from the world. The problem was I was full of experiments but very little experience. I listened to and was led by the preacher, teacher, prophet and priest, doctor, lawyer, and Indian chief; but I was not being led by Holy Spirit. Experimenting means I heard the Truth and quite possibly acknowledged the Truth. I may even have understood the Truth to some degree, but I refused to walk out the Truth I heard, and; consequently, I had no experience to build my faith.

How many times have you heard this quote? "…And the truth shall set you free…" I have heard it in movies, at work, school, church; every born-again believer seems to have heard it or have at some point thought or recited these six words. The problem is that it is a misquote. No matter how many people quote it, it is still a misquote. You see the Bible actually says: "And you will **know** the Truth, and the Truth will set you free" (John 8:32 AMP, emphasis added).

The word "and" lets me know that there was something before this sentence. So I did some investigating (meaning I read the whole chapter) and here is what took place. The Lord was preaching and answering questions in the Temple court. As He spoke, there were people present that believed in Him. The Word of God says: "As He said these things, many believed in Him [trusted, relied on, and adhered to Him]" (John 8:30 AMP).

Not all, but "many" believed in Him. To THESE Jews, (the ones that believed, trusted, relied on, and adhered to Him) He spoke. "So Jesus said to those Jews who had believed in Him, If you abide in My word [hold fast to My teachings and live in accordance with them], you are truly My disciples" (John 8:31 AMP).

Christ only deals with those that acknowledge Him as Lord. He is crystal clear with His words. If I abide in His word, meaning to hold fast to what He teaches and tells as I read, get understanding and hear from Holy Spirit and then live according to that Word, then I can say that I am a disciple. After I hold fast to and apply what I have learned into my life, I shall, according to the Greek word ginōskō, "Know," meaning "to understand and to perceive", the Truth (Strong's Greek Concordance #1097).

The definition of the English word "know" is "to have a familiarity or grasp of, as through study or experience." It is also defined "to be acquainted or familiar with" (Collins English Dictionary).

The Lord revealed to me that as I hear His words, which are Truth (whether through the Bible or my prayer closet), and I do as

He asks of me, I can observe Holy Spirit working in me and on my behalf. This helps me develop a deeper relationship with Him. As I spend time with Him, and become familiar with His ways, and become the Lord's friend, I experience these Truths by "walking them out." THEN I can say, He knows me and to *the degree* I willingly walk out what He has revealed that I "know" Him.

"And you will know the Truth, and the Truth will set you free" (John 8:32 AMP).

What can set you free? The Truth you "know." Not the Truth you read, not the Truth you watch, not the Truth that is preached to you. Christ said if you adhere to what HE says to you (through whatever medium), then you are experiencing Truth and the Truth you know (through experience) will set you free; not experimenting with doctrines or church activities. All the fancy preaching, stage props, eloquent speaking and word rhyming has zero value if you do not get a Rhema Word from the Lord and then "walk ye in it." This leads into an understanding of His Reality. The Reality that being willing and obedient to act upon what you hear will lead you to eating the good of the land. To be obedient, you must first hear.

The Lord can speak through many sources. His favorite of course is Holy Spirit in you. He also can be manifested through people, elders, pastors, etc. He can even use a donkey. That is not the point. "But He said, Blessed (happy and to be envied) rather are those who hear the Word of God and obey and practice it!" (Luke 11:28 AMP).

Was I getting any direct Word from God? Was I putting it to practice? Was I seeking more of Him through prayer and relationship with Holy Spirit? Did I wake up and ask Him what to wear, what to eat, how to drive to work? Was I allowing Him to be Lord of all; or was He really not Lord at all? If I were not walking it out for myself, then I had zero, zilch, nada, of experience because I had a deficit in my relationship with Him. I was only experimenting.

Once again I will quote Holy Spirit as He spoke in the book of Hebrews: "For even though by this time you ought to be teaching others, you actually need someone **to teach you over again the very first principles of God's Word.** You have come to need milk, not solid food. For everyone who continues to feed on milk is **obviously inexperienced** *and* unskilled in the doctrine of righteousness (of conformity to the divine will in purpose, thought, and action), **for he is a mere infant** [not able to talk yet]!" (Hebrews 5:12-13 AMP).

I lacked experience; I was holding on to my old life. I needed to be taught the most basic of principles. I was born-again in spirit. I need to follow the lead of Holy Spirit so I can learn how to be an ambassador of my true Kingdom. I desired to build relationship with God as my Father. This takes time; it takes commitment. Why did I still feel so trapped? Why did I still feel imprisoned?

My spiritual growth was suffocated in a room called experimenting. The gag in my mouth was called pride. My ears were full of the sounds of religion. My hands were tied by disobedience. The lock on the door read doubt. My shackles were fashioned by my un-renewed soul (mind), and my flesh was nothing but a puppet. The prison had already been opened over 2,000 years ago. I had chosen to close the door on myself due to lack of revelation, and all the windows were blocked by bars labeled fear. The door can only be opened from the inside, and the key is labeled faith. The key is only found in my prayer closet. It reads "Relationship with Holy Spirit."

It took faith for me to walk out of the room. Staying in the room looks good; I go to the right services, I know the right songs, I can quote scripture, the pastors know me by name, I tithe, and I volunteer! Experimenting with the Christian walk looks so good. Stepping out in faith and seeking His will for me daily, even hourly, as I experience His guidance and learn from my failures as well as His victories in me… THAT looks God.

"A man with one experience stands far above a man with a bag full of experiments" Daniel Isaiah

Chapter 8

Ministry vs. Majesty

"And then I will say to them openly (publicly), I never knew you; depart from Me, you who act wickedly [disregarding My commands]" (Matthew 7:23 AMP).

If I look at the way ministry is defined, as a "doing a work for the church" then I can say I have been in "ministry" for many years. I was serving in churches, teaching Bible studies, serving in this church group or that church group. I have given out water, fed the homeless, etc. Hindsight being twenty-twenty, I have stayed busy in doing, preparing for, or going to ministry most of my early years in Christ. This is what I was taught ministry was. This is what comes to mind when most people think of the word "ministry." It is in this misunderstanding that I was kept captive. How could ministry hold me back from God you ask? It can and will when not done in Him.

Early in 2009 I had come to realize that I was very busy in ministry. I felt the Lord asking me to draw back and stay still. So one day in prayer, I asked the Lord how many of the speaking engagements I had the prior year that were not of Him and how many were in His will. I heard Holy Spirit say "Three."

So I thought "Wow; three, not bad." I had gone to only three that were not of Him. He corrected me and said "No, I only sent you to three. The rest you went out on your own." That was a hard thing to hear, and is to this day a harder thing to admit.

This chapter will speak about the real Ministry. The same ministry that started in the Garden of Eden and the one that Jesus Christ practiced. This chapter will discuss the only type of ministry that matters and the only thing the Lord cares about.

At its most basic level, this ministry I speak of is directed only to the Lord and what we were created for. The "other" ministry is for man and towards man. That ministry towards man has its place, but it is secondary to our created purpose. Now mind you, I understand that many minister to others "in the name of Jesus Christ" and that is awesome. Unfortunately, not all that are out there ministering have taken the time to truly minister to the Lord first and to Him alone.

*******NOW HERE IS A WARNING*******
I do not want anyone to read into this. I am NOT saying "to serve is not Christ-like." I am NOT saying "do not serve." I am strictly speaking of being mindful of substituting intimate relationship with Holy Spirit with actions or involvement in a church, group, or ministry to others. Please feel free to serve as you believe with all your heart you are led by God. My only question to Christians is; "Do you believe with all your heart that what you are doing is of the Lord?"

This may be the most difficult chapter to read, but it can also be the most fruitful if you pray over these illuminations and seek Him for deeper revelation.

I am His Temple

We are going to do a comparison of the old Temple of the Lord and the "New" Temple of the Lord so we can better understand our purpose. When Jesus Christ walked among us in the flesh, the Temple building of God was known to be a beautiful and majestic structure. It was approximately four and a half football fields long. It took over forty-six years to build and was the focus of every Jew who worshipped God. It was made up of three parts; the Holy of Holies, the Inner Court and the Outer Court.

Holy of Holies

The Holy of Holies was the most sacred place for a Jew. It was in the Temple of God, and only a High Priest could enter and make atonement for Israel once a year on Yom Kippur or the Day of Atonement. This was where God was ministered to. Here is where God was satisfied. This took an act of faith on the high priest's part. He had to know his own sins were atoned for and that what he was bringing before the Lord was in accordance to the Lord's standards and requests. He had to come mentally correct, and his focus had to be on God and God alone. There was no fanfare here nor any type of show; it was quiet and still. Just the priest, the sacrifice, the articles needed, and of course, the presence of the Lord. Behind a big veil, no one could see him, but God; it was private, secluded, and intimate. That's how the Lord likes it.

The Inner Court

The Inner Court was the place of preparation, which was reserved for the men of Israel, to prepare the priest to enter into the presence of the Lord in the Holy of Holies. It was also the place of teaching and discourse where the experts and Rabbis would gather to discuss the sacred book of Judaism, consisting of the Torah, the Prophets, and the Hebrew Scriptures also known as the Tenach. Here, they could also instruct young men in the Torah and the Hebraic laws.

The Outer Court

The Outer Court was where the priest would come out and meet the people. In those days, the Sons of Korah would stand in the Outer Court on the steps of the Gate and sing the psalms and praises of the Lord to Jew and Gentile alike. Here, the priests would gather the sacrifices for people. They would meet and greet; they would serve the people, and it was where Jesus Christ could be seen often ministering to all that would draw near to Him.

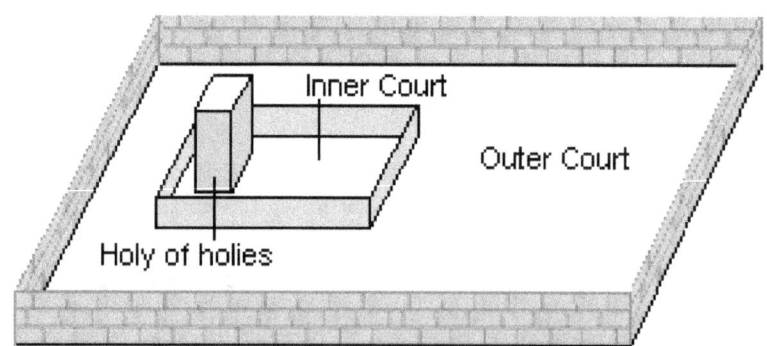

Why is this important to know? Understanding that we are now the Temple of the Lord will help free us from strongholds that want to keep us with an identity to self.

The Lord made a statement one day to a group of people that were trying to get some physical proof of whom He (Jesus Christ) was in the Spiritual.

According to the scripture, "Then the Jews retorted, What sign can You show us, seeing You do these things? [What sign, miracle, token, indication can You give us as evidence that You have authority and are commissioned to act in this way?]. Jesus answered them, Destroy (undo) this temple, and in three days I will raise it up again. Then the Jews replied, It took forty-six years to build this temple (sanctuary), and will You raise it up in three days? But He had spoken of the temple which was His body" (John 2:18-21 AMP)

Verse twenty-one lets us know what He meant by "temple." This was not revealed to the disciples themselves, however, until *after* His resurrection. "When therefore He had risen from the dead, His disciples remembered that He said this. And so they believed and trusted and relied on the Scripture and the word (message) Jesus had spoken" (John 2:22 AMP).

Once again we find ourselves in an area where definition of words is crucial to revelation of meaning. In the Gospel of John chapter two, we have two different words for temple. Earlier in the Gospel verses fourteen and fifteen Jesus Christ cleaned out the Temple. The Greek word used in these verses is "hieron," which refers to the temple as a whole (Strong's Greek Concordance #2411). Actually, it was the Outer Court of the temple which Jesus cleansed.

Now the word Jesus Himself uses in verse nineteen and is repeated and affirmed by the Jews in verse twenty is not hieron but is instead "naos" which means "shrine and sanctuary: and it is the word which the Jews used when referring to the inner sanctuary of the temple" (Strong's Greek concordance #3485).

This same word has been used in reference to the body by Paul in 1 Corinthians 6:19 when he says that the holy place today is not a temple made with hands but that our body is the temple (naos) of the Holy Spirit.

When I was born again, Holy Spirit came to live inside of me; I became God's shrine and sanctuary in my spirit. Paul shares with us the following: "Do you not discern *and* understand that you [the whole church at Corinth] are God's temple (His sanctuary), and that God's Spirit has His permanent dwelling in you [to be at home in you, collectively as a church and **also individually**]?" (1 Corinthians 3:16 AMP, emphasis added).

This was my Father keeping His integrity. He promised all that are born-again forgiveness of our sins, as well as, a new birth and HIS Spirit living in us. He said: "Then will I sprinkle clean water upon you, and **you shall be clean from all your uncleanness**; and from all your idols will I cleanse you. A new heart will I give you **and a new spirit will I put within you**, and I will take away the stony heart out of your flesh and give you a heart of flesh. And **I will put my Spirit within you** and cause you to walk in My statutes, and you shall heed My ordinances and do them" (Ezekiel 36:25-27 AMP, emphasis added).

Many believers can express to one degree or another that their sins have been forgiven, and they will be with the Lord Jesus Christ one day. That all sounds good, but God has so much more planned for us in our salvation. The Lord came so I could have Life (Zoë) and Life in abundance (John 10:10). Due to poor teaching, and lack of understanding, many (like myself at one point), are stuck at the foot of the cross never realizing there is more to this walk and this journey on the other side of the cross. He would like to lead us on to the resurrected life, on the side where we are being led and controlled by Holy Spirit, on the side where Jesus wants to lead us besides still waters and green pastures (Psalm 23:2). He wants us on the side where we enter His Reality and leave that tomb where it belongs; in a slowly fading memory.

From tomb to tent; from tent to Temple

Before my new birth, I was dead in a fleshly tomb, trapped in my sins and worthy of death. The Lord came and died in my place; which allows God to see me as a righteous child based on Christ's sacrifice. He then rose again to give me an expectancy of the same.

Furthermore, He gifted me with a measure of faith so I could be birthed into a new Kingdom as a new creation, and finally, He sealed me with His very same Holy Spirit. Holy Spirit was deposited in my spirit, in me so I could be a Temple, an inner sanctuary, a Holy of Holies with the presence of God living in ME.

This would allow me to grow up into Christ-likeness as I was led past the cross from faith to faith into my new Kingdom lifestyle (Romans 1:17). Yet I popped a tent, so to speak, and stayed at the foot of the cross. I became complacent with talking about the work He did; always looking back at the tomb He freed me from and going back into that darkness from time to time so I could wallow in a past that belonged to a dead person. All the while I was ignoring that He had come down off the cross and that His desire was for me to follow His lead beyond the cross, into a Kingdom lifestyle and take my place as the Temple (naos) of Holy Spirit (God); just like Christ was here on earth.

I was freed from a tomb, and I am meant to be a Temple, but I decided to abide in a tent instead. As a "tent-dweller," I stayed at the foot of the cross and did not venture past being "saved." Living in a tent had many drawbacks. I was concerned that the next strong wind that blew would remove my tent and expose my nakedness. I wondered if the fire would go out because it was cold outside. I would open my eyes in the darkness hoping that the sun would rise soon and shine some light so that I could see. I was concerned for my food, and I kept an eye on the water supply.

Then one day as I prayed He said to me, "Your tent is crippling your transformation, and in many ways, it is worse than the tomb I saved you from."

I asked "Why, Lord?"

He replied, "Because, in the tomb, you could not know Me. You were far from Me stuck in a prison of flesh and soul, a slave to lies the enemy planted in you. I reached down to free you and make you My Temple, and you are choosing to stay in a tent, shaking, unsure, fearful. Using false bravado and a religious lifestyle as dried up fig leaves to hide your lack of relationship with me."

I wept. I was a king deciding to live as a pauper. I was a son refusing to accept my inheritance. Sadly, my own lifestyle was helping others be comfortable in their own tents. I was an example of how NOT TO live a Kingdom lifestyle. I wept more; my body shook, and as I bathed in His mercy, He fed me Grace, I drank from His love, and then He washed my mind with His Word.

I got up just as I was, but with a revelation that was causing internal battles to take place. I was in a state of rebellion against my old nature. I was in the midst of a revolution and Christ was leading the charge! I didn't need to be concerned about strong winds, for I am a Temple of God and I abide in Him, and He abides in me.

Nothing can move me. The fire outside was not my source of heat or comfort because I had a burning Fire in me that kept me warm from the inside out and it is my source of confidence. He is my daily Bread and I hunger not. My water supply is Holy Spirit and He streams from inside me like rivers of living water.

As these things played over and over in my spirit, as He unveiled them to me, I saw the Son rise in me and I had light to get up and be led by Him, to the other side of the Cross, to His Kingdom; on earth as it is in Heaven (Luke 11:2). I never looked back at that tomb; I never bothered to take down the tent, and I just followed Him when He said "Come." I was not sure what He had in store, but I was done with tombs and tents, I only desired to be His temple and let Him have free reign.

Ministry in the Temple to His Majesty

As I started to look at my walk with the Lord, I realized my distractions were nothing new. I was not the only one that was fascinated with staying busy and I was not the only person to ignore Him.

In Ezekiel 44:9-26 the Lord is speaking to Israel. He addresses a group of Levite priests. There were two types of temple attendants that God was dealing with. One group was more concerned about the Outer Court living and pleasing the crowds. Addressing issues, taking care of sacrifices, getting recognition, feeding those that came, teaching; all in the **Outer Court**. My focus today is not on them per se but on the other group. The other group were the ones that when they saw the Outer Court falling into ruins decided to do what was most important to God, and that was take care of the **Inner Court** and minister to Him.

The group was called the Sons of Zadok. Why does that matter to you? The sons of Zadok were selected to minister to the Lord because they "kept the charge" of the sanctuary when the children of Israel went astray from the Lord and worshipped idols. When the Outer Court was defiled they were determined and focused *on maintaining the sanctity and wholeness of the Inner Court.*

Today, I find that many in the church confuse knowing about God with actually knowing God. Knowing about God can be done by reading the Bible, knowing God can only be done by spending time with Him, and Him alone. You cannot love someone unless you know them. You cannot know someone unless you spend intimate quality time with them. This is what the Lord said in Ezekiel.

"But the Levites who went far away from Me when Israel went astray, who went astray from Me **after their idols**, they shall bear [the punishment for] their iniquity *and* guilt. They shall minister in My sanctuary, having oversight as guards at the gates of the temple and ministering in the temple. They shall slay the burnt offering and the sacrifice **for the people**, and they shall **attend the people to serve them**. **Because** [the priests] ministered to [the people] before their idols and became a **stumbling block** of iniquity *and* guilt to the house of Israel, therefore I have lifted up My hand *and* have sworn against them, says the Lord God, that they shall bear the punishment for their iniquity *and* guilt. And they **shall not come near to Me** to do the office of a priest to Me, nor come near to any of My holy things that are most sacred; but they shall bear their shame *and* their punishment for the abominations which they have committed. Yet I will appoint them as caretakers to have charge of the temple, for all the service of the temple and for all that will be done in it. **But the Levitical priests, the sons of Zadok, who kept the charge of My sanctuary when the children of Israel went astray from Me, shall come near to Me to minister to Me, and they shall attend Me to offer to Me the fat and the blood, says the Lord God. They shall enter into My sanctuary; and they shall come near to My table to minister to Me, and they shall keep My charge.** When they enter the gates of the Inner Court, they shall be clothed in linen garments; no wool shall be on them while they minister at the gates of the Inner Court and within the temple. They shall have linen turbans on their heads and linen breeches upon their loins; **they shall not gird themselves with anything that causes [them to] sweat**" (Ezekiel 44:10-18 AMP, emphasis added).

I was so active in the church and doing church things that I was kept busy, and I realize now that in busyness is a barrenness that cannot produce fruit of the Spirit. I was so busy ministering to the people that I forgot about Him who came to give Life.

In my initial walk with the Lord, I was told to read my Bible, starting in Psalms, then someone else said to read John and someone else said to begin reading Romans while another said that the best thing for me to do was to pray in the morning or maybe at night. I was also told to join the men's group to grow, and the Bible study group to know, and the volunteer group to show; and I did it ALL. I was a Christian! I was serving others; I was a Christian. That is the basic formula for churches today, get them in, get them saved, get them involved and make them a part of the church. Many desire Christ fellowship, yet fellowship with Christ is ironically the last thing that happens. You see, if someone thinks of God as a boss, then the answer to getting closer to Him is more work. If someone sees Him as a teacher, well then the answer to getting closer to Him is to read, learn, and memorize more. When you see Him as Father, and see yourself as the one He birthed, you begin a relationship that leads to knowing Him as such. A precious, personal, powerful relationship.

One winter day I came to my Father asking why, I was feeling far from Him. He revealed through Holy Spirit the following. The formula from man and religion is: "Get involved in ministry, this is your destiny and will bring you closer to His majesty."

The formula from God is: "Get closer to MY Majesty, this is your ONLY Destiny, and I through you will do Ministry."

In all honesty, there is very little distinction between serving the church and serving the Lord Jesus Christ. There is also very little distinction between the word recreation and the word recreation. Recreation is for fun, and re-creation is me being re-created into the image of Christ. Both words look the same; the difference is this; one is lived while the other is an illusion. The Lord told me that many in the Church live for recreation time, which is a vacation from the world. Ironically, re-creation was the vocation He called us to so we could overcome the world so we would not need a vacation. Why would we? We are meant to bring Heaven to earth. Which one are you pursuing?

Many who will read this book have done their very best to serve the body, to save sinners and focus on helping the church. I was there, and then one day I asked myself; "Have I been focused on serving those around me? Or have I been focused on serving the Lord? Am I church and ministry led, or Spirit led?"

In Ezekiel 44:15 it is made clear the two preparatory things we must do to minister to the Lord. "Draw near" and "stand before Me." Anything else I do is in vain until I first draw near to Him and stand before Him.

I looked at my own walk and realized that ministry to Him first was not the basis for everything I was doing. I was attempting to fit Him into my busy schedule. I forgot that the Lord of the work *is more important* than the work of the Lord.

Let me be transparent. Working for the Lord has an amazing attraction to the flesh. I loved being busy helping and serving the church. I would go speak, and be rewarded with seeing satisfied faces and smiles, tears of joy, or tears from breakthroughs and the laughter after a revelation. Staying at home just did not seem attractive to me. I could serve the Lord though and feel accomplishment, and satisfaction. I looked good, BUT I did not look like a son to God. I was not being led by Holy Spirit (Romans 8:14).

The Word of God tells me that my flesh has a nature of its own; desires of its own and impulses all to itself. One of those is looking good, especially in ministry. I became aware that much of the work being done in the name of the Lord was not ministry to Him at all! Based on words taken out of context from the Bible, some justify going forth and acting without Him. The Lord Himself has told us about the class of Levites who busily served the Temple but did not serve God. They served the house and not the Master of the House. Service to the Lord and service to the Body appear almost identical, and is in the flesh, arduous to antithesize.

One thing that I pray about is the subterfuge that darkness has involved many...oh so many of us in. Many of us go out and bring sinners into salvation through belief in the Lord Jesus Christ. Others help build up the believers in the knowledge of the Word; yet how many are ministering to the Lord Himself? The desire to "serve" is found in the flesh. It is a desire to look good and, therefore, is a natural way of doing things. The flesh enjoys being busy, doing things and proving how much it has learned, can do, and will do... ALL of this regardless of how "good" it looks, does not look GOD if He is not the one directing us. We may give the illusion we are serving sinners, or serving believers, but all the while if **we** choose to serve the so called "church" we are serving only the flesh and sadly...that is our focus: the church, sinners and believers, and not God Himself.

What do I mean by serving God or serving the Church? The Word of God says: "They shall enter into **My sanctuary**; and they shall come near to **My table** to **minister to Me**, and they shall **keep My charge**" (Ezekiel 44:16 AMP, emphasis added).

*** NEWS FLASH! *** His sanctuary is not your local church; you are the temple of the Holy Spirit that He sent back so we can have a relationship with Him. The main ministry that the Lord desires is YOU drawing near to the Lord in spirit and standing quietly before Him. This is easier said than done. I had trouble praying and standing still. Even when I was in my prayer closet, my soul would wander to external issues. I had an ability to lead, and partner with others to DO many things for God. Yet drawing near and standing still was a chore. Praying for 15 minutes felt like an hour, an hour a day, a day a week. I had to be aggressive with my soul and flesh. I have yet to meet anyone that ministers and serves the Lord that does not understand fully and appreciate the unique relationship and sweet time spent when He wakes you up in the middle of the night to pray and spend time with Him. Unless you know what it is like to draw near to God, you cannot know what it is to serve Him.

Drawing near is only done in spirit, not soul and certainly never flesh. Trying to stand in the soul realm and flesh is choosing to stand far from God. Standing far from Him makes it impossible to minister much less serve Him. He cannot be served from a distance. Can a man water a flower in his garden while standing in another city? The only place that ministry to the Lord is possible is in our prayer closet. As we invest real time with Him He will speak as we hear and learn to distinguish His voice, we choose to obey; as we willingly obey, He reveals more of Himself, and we grow in relationship. He wants us to seek to know Him personally and intimately by spending time with Him in His presence, like we would do on a long dinner date, not superficially as in a drive-thru pick up window. He does not want to date me either. His death on the cross was more than an act of Love…it was a proposal. He will not relent until we are all His.

I was stuck in the Outer Court. The Outer Court represents the lunches, the BBQ's, the small groups, movie nights, and busyness of religion. All of this involves other people. Nonetheless, it is in the quietness of the Holy Place, my prayer closet, where I approach God. Today's world is meant to keep me from Him, with cell phones that text and show movies and play games, with social media outlets and the need to post pictures and look good, Christians are distracted with things they need not be involved in.

People are in constant motion; fascinated with the watching of scripted reality television, concerned about who dies off on what show, and who posted what on some social media page. Then the desire to preach, teach and show-off what they have learned from a book, a pastor or a video online without first walking it out takes the place of God. It gives an illusion of relationship.

The modern Christian CANNOT STAND STILL! The amount of things associating our soul realm with the world system is colossal. There is a plethora of stimuli for my flesh. From porn in private to posting online publicly, from funny video websites to the need to star in fifteen second videos. Constantly trying to get exposure to SELF. All these serve one purpose...keeping me prisoner to an illusion and away from ministry to the Lord, so I do not come to know Him as Father. It is all Outer Court ministry.

A mature spiritual person can stop. He/she can stand still. They can delete that social media account; they can stop posting all those pictures of themselves. They can function without the phone glued to their hand. They choose God over man. Reality over illusions, he/she can stand still and await orders. Those that claim to be leaders WILL be held responsible for what they teach and how they lead God's children towards ministry to Him or away from Him by not teaching them the Truth. The former can only be done by being a living example of someone who knows he/she is a Temple.

It grieves me to see my brothers and sisters in Christ go to church to hear the latest popular man/woman of God speak because of who he/she may be. They want to hear the latest hottest message, they desire to be in the new, hip, church and have it known to all they speak to. They get a word from man and feel like they just won the lottery, they follow pastors and not Christ. They wouldn't know Christ if He sat next to them at church. They want the quick message without any change in their relationship with God. They have no internal change, and if nothing changes well then; nothing changes.

For a Christian, there is only ONE sin before God; Disobedience to Him. This sin is manifested in two ways: First, hearing His voice and NOT obeying Him. This is rebellion. Second, is going ahead of Him when He did not tell me to. This is a presumption. Not doing what He has asked you to do and also acting on your own is EQUALLY offensive to God. I have asked dozens of Christians, especially rap and song artists if they have heard from the Lord. They all say, "Yes." Yet many times, the Lord says to me, "What they are doing is not of Me."

Are you a "sent one" or a "went one?" Many go out on their gifting, and yet they were never sent by Him who gives the gifts.

Many have used familiar excuses; "My pastor told me; someone said…; I felt that…; I heard…" and yet it was nothing but their own soul-realm or darkness working through others who had the "good" intentions of sending them out. The outcome is that they **WENT** out on their own with no authority rather than being **SENT** out by God. I know many that feel they are sent to sing, rap and minister at places for the Lord, and sadly, they are not. They go on their own. The Lord is calling them to draw closer to Him, but "doing" ministry is much more important to them than standing still and listening. Sadly, they will never be SENT until they learn to be still and submit. That takes faith, and faith is built through relationship with Him, and relationship with Him comes only by spending a good quantity of quality time alone with Him, and maturing in spirit.

    Some of the questions I asked myself were: "How much have I done that I heard Him actually tell me to do?" and "How much have I done just based on how GOOD it looks or because the church or a church member invited, asked or told me to?" Looking good destroys our ability to look God. So many want to "look good" and have that feeling of accomplishment in the Lord. They spend their time doing that one "good" thing; not knowing that the one "good" thing is getting in the way of what the Lord wants to do in them.

    We are not discussing evil things but the good things. The "good" things present themselves, quietly, and feed our strongholds a diet of deceptions. Like a snake in the grass, that "good" thing becomes a vice grip that holds me back from knowing God. You may think: "How can THIS be wrong?" You may say that what you are doing is the "good" thing. I ask you; did you check first with your Lord? Did you inquire from the one you call your God? And if yes…what did HE answer?

    I know as His child; I should not do evil things. The issue is when my soul, that has been trained to be independent by the world, (translation for a Christian = independent from God), and self-reliant, (translation = reliant on self), tells me that something is "good". At that moment I "reason" that it must be okay; I convince myself that I should do it. While it is true that the thing you are pondering may actually be a "good thing," you must take the next step to ask if it is a GOD thing.

    When the Lord said "They shall stand before me," that means I go before Him and STAND STILL and do NOT move until HE says "Go!" (Ezekiel 44:15 KJV). And if I do not hear His voice, my focus should be on building that relationship so I can hear; it should never be on doing something. The doing comes after the "be-ing," and the "be-ing" means being still in His presence so He can speak and tell me what He wants me to know, do, speak, share, pray, get rid of, defend, cut out, let go, hold on to, or bless. In this, and only this, can we say that we minister to the Lord. In the Outer Court, we are busy ministering to the people: we share the Gospel; we feed the homeless; we cook for the pastor; we clean the church; we volunteer on worship teams; we bake brownies and we attend bake sales. In the Outer Court, it is fleshly human needs that govern. This was how the priests were kept busy in the Outer Court in the book of Ezekiel. If someone needed to sacrifice an ox or sheep, (translation for us today = needs prayer, has a concern, needs counseling, a lift to church, etc.) there is work for me to do, the "Outer Court minister" in me is satisfied.

In the Holiest of Holies, there is no one but Holy Spirit and you. When I pull aside to listen to God, it is His Spirit that lives in us, that is speaking in a still small quiet voice. It takes me being still, quieting my soul realm (mind), to hear Him. It is just me and Holy Spirit. No one else. In this Kingdom, He is the only thing that matters. If he says "Daniel go do this," I do it. Regardless of how small or grand. If I receive no Word from Him, I do nothing. Ministry unto the Lord is a SPIRIT THING. Because God is Spirit and those that worship Him MUST do so in spirit. So when I approach God, it cannot be with anything but spirit. Real ministry is "unto me" says the Lord. In the inner sanctuary, in spirit (Ezekiel 44:16). It is where NO ONE can see.

The hardest thing I have ever had to do is stand still and minister to my Father, yet it has been the most rewarding and humbling experience. In today's world, I have seen countless amounts of wasted energy in working for the Lord. How can one minister to people when one has not learned to minister to the Lord? How can one run around being busy, giving hours, and days, weeks and months to the Outer Court and not give God at least the same amount of time ministering to Him? How much time do I spend with friends or family yet are not giving the same amount of time to God. Shouldn't the ratio at least be two to one, with two representing time with Him? THAT is where true relationship comes from.

Let's look at a natural example: If you were married, and your spouse spent 97% of their time doing things, working, buying you food, looking good by working out for you, baking for you, reading books on relationships to be a better spouse etc…and only had 3% of their time left to give you and even THAT time your spouse was distracted mentally; how would you feel? How would you respond if they said "I am doing all of this for you."

Oh, how I offer up my pleas before the Lord: "Lord search me! Lord reveal to me, Lord I confess I have started ministries without YOUR approval, I have gone to performances WITHOUT YOUR SENDING ME, I have prayed for, helped out at, gave an opinion WITHOUT YOU, and I want nothing more than for you to lead me...Lord I will wait for you! I will wait for you to lead me, and I will focus on hearing only from you. I choose to stand still OVER looking good! In Jesus name, I pray Amen!"

Is there a time and place to serve? Absolutely! Matthew 25 addresses the value of ministry, but note that those being rewarded were not even aware of the ministry that they had performed when they were getting recognition for their ministry in Heaven. There is nothing wrong with serving others, as long as HE was served first and HE sent you out. There is a work for God to the people, and it has to be done. As much as the Lord desires it, He cannot secure everyone to minister and serve Him. This takes Christians focused on God, and God alone, with intent to become Christ-like as they minister to Him. This takes time. My Apostle told me that when I come to the Lord I need to get rid of two things; my calendar and my watch. I am on God's time and in God's Agenda. My only focus should be to not hinder my growth by disobedience or running ahead as I draw nearer to Him. Amen?

For many, there is a natural reluctance to leave the thrill and excitement of the Outer Court, the stage presence and the applause of knowing they did a good thing. They focus on serving people; leaving the Lord standing by Himself in their lives, waiting for the moment when He can have a relationship with them, waiting so He can share what He has to say about their lives and the direction HE wants them to go. Why did He choose the Sons of Zadok? Because when the children of Israel went astray, they (the Sons of Zadok) recognized that the Outer Court had been corrupted, so they did not seek to preserve it. Instead, they made it their business to preserve the sanctity of the Holy Place, the sanctuary of God Himself.

The Word of God says that we are His temple. As you look at the picture that follows, you can see how the Temple structure can be used to illustrate how God uniquely designed us to be His Temple. When the Lord said He was the "Temple" HE did not mean the building He meant the actual holding vessel of Holy Spirit. Are YOU aware of your "Temple" status?

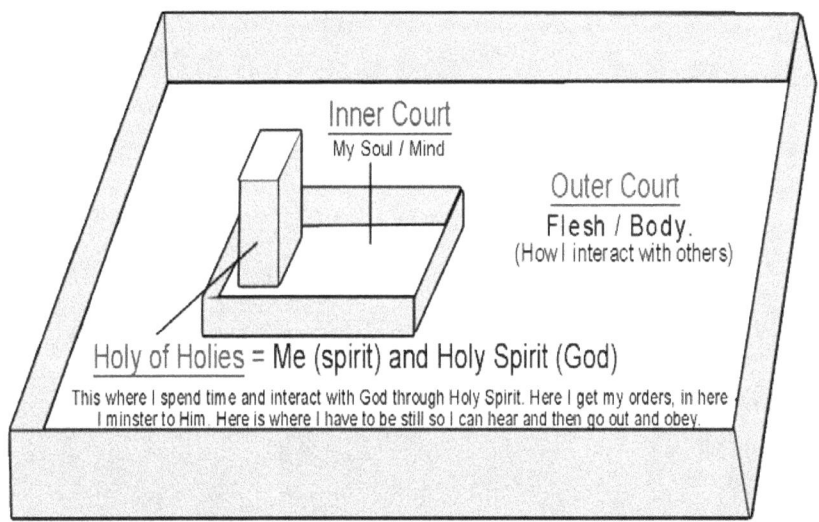

The Outer Court, FLESH, is where you deal with and address others, especially those the Lord would send you to serve. This is also where we stay busy, if not watchful in the spirit.

The Inner Court, SOUL/MIND, serves a dual purpose; it is where we prepare ourselves to minister to God as we are transformed by its renewing (Romans 12:2) and where we cast down all things through Christ that oppose Him as Lord (2 Corinthians 10:5). In here, we develop His thoughts and His views as we follow the spirit's instructions.

Then we have the Holiest of Holies, our SPIRIT with HOLY SPIRIT; it is here that we are in His presence. Here, we come and stand still; we lean in, listen to and learn about God as we minister to Him. It is in here where we realize His majesty firsthand, where His Love can fill us and flow from us; it is where we are one. THIS is our purpose. In here, He trains us up as sons, not good sons but God sons. It was, and STILL is, the Holy of Holies that God wants to set apart and preserve for Him. He wants your spirit to be built up into maturity. Not influenced by Outer Court distractions.

As you read this, I would ask that you leave the Outer Court, prepare your Inner Court with His promises, and proceed into that

Holy Place in quiet prayer and contemplation. Here is where we get the words of Life; one on one with God… that is His desire. Amen?

Chapter 9

Getting out of the way

"New nature creates new appetites."
Rev. Williams (my spiritual Dad)

I constantly hear Christians quote these words from John 3:16; "For God so Loved the world that he gave…" How many have also pondered "for the Son so Loved the Father?"

Not many realize that it is Jesus, the Christ Himself, speaking these words and prophesying of His own death and resurrection. He was well aware of how life was going to be for Him and yet He still held on to one thing, and one thing only, His Father's will.

Many Christians run on bios; what feels good and gives external satisfaction. Many still run on psyche, what I have read and learned from man (this includes Biblical teaching) and what I perceive to be reality based on my former father's (satan) teaching. There is a group that is not busy in the Outer Court. There is a group that has set up the Inner Court with the promises of God who cast down every imagination that would raise itself up against the Christ-likeness being built up in them. This group enters into the Holy of Holies through dedicated prayer time, dedicated Word time, and through the fine tuning of hearing God speak through Holy Spirit in their inner man (spirit), and then, they go out and obey. These were once called the Sons of Zadok in the Old Testament, but now God calls those that hear HIS voice through Holy Spirit and follow…SONS. "For as many as are led by the Spirit of God, they are the sons of God" (Romans 8:14 KJV).

The Lord Himself, when questioned why He did what He did, answered; "I assure you, most solemnly I tell you, the **Son** is able to do **nothing of Himself** (of His own accord); but He is able **to do only** what He sees the Father doing, for whatever the Father does is what the Son does in the same way [in His turn]" (John 5:19

AMP, emphasis added).

The Lord said He did nothing that originated from Himself. Fleshly desires would not dictate how He obeyed His Father; His soul realm had nothing to contribute to the Father's plans. He had an intimate relationship, and in this relationship He knew the Father well. He saw how the Father did things and when it was His turn He did the same. Not before…when He was told to, and as He saw it done. The example was His Father. We as Christians need to have an intimate relationship with Holy Spirit. Holy Spirit will train us and guide us into Christ-likeness. As God becomes Father to us, and we see Him move in our lives, through others, and through His supernatural power, we can in our turn, comfort and supply to others as He leads us; not going ahead of Him, not waiting behind Him, instead, just letting Christ work through us.

Even our speech needs to be spiritually led. The Lord Himself spoke only as led.

"**I am able to do nothing from Myself** [independently, of My own accord—but only as I am taught by God and as I get His orders]. **Even as I hear**, I judge [I decide as I am bidden to decide. As the voice comes to Me, so I give a decision], and My judgment is right (just, righteous), **because I do not seek or consult My own will** [I have no desire to do what is pleasing to Myself, My own aim, My own purpose] but only the will and pleasure of the Father Who sent Me" (John 5:30 AMP, emphasis added).

There were only two things that stopped me from growing in the Lord. I had two idols that I refused to deal with. These two idols are difficult to throw out. The Lord is clear as to what they are.

"Therefore speak to them and say to them, Thus says the Lord God: Every man of the house of Israel who takes **his idols** [of **self-will** and **unsubmissiveness**] into his heart and puts the stumbling block of his iniquity [idols of silver and gold] before his face, and yet comes to the prophet [to inquire of him], I the Lord will answer him, answer him according to the multitude of his idols" (Ezekiel 14:4 AMP, emphasis added).

I refused to submit to the Lord. I refused to have His will be done. I wanted to feel good, live well and look good. In my refusing to pray earnestly, (not just rambling off a wish list), in my refusing to shut up and learn to pray in the spirit and with Holy Spirit, in my refusing to listen to the Lord in my quiet time and my refusing to build a real relationship with God as He spoke and I kept His charge,

I chose bios (flesh) and psyche (soul/mind) life over the True Life. I had a new nature but was not feeding the new appetite. The only person stopping my relationship with God was myself...and I had to get out of the way!

I dropped out of Religious University, which is affiliated with the World View curriculum. I started taking classes at Holy Spirit University; they are accredited by Heaven Inc. I wanted to excel in "Super-Natural Kingdom Living 101," "Spirit Speaking 101," "Holy Ghost Listening 101" and "Christ-likeness" as my major. I knew when I signed up that I was going to be a Lifetime student. It didn't matter to me; I loved the classes and the tuition was already paid for over 2,000 years ago. I just had to make a decision and enroll. Where did I start? It started with my prayer time.

Getting my knees bruised

One of my new appetites was for prayer. After all, Jesus continually pulled aside to pray. He encourages prayer and He constantly went up to speak to His Father. So why would I choose not to follow His example? Now mind you, it is not easy at first. It takes a good four to six weeks to get into the flow and adjust in your flesh and soul to this new habit. God will honor you in this time of adjustment. He knows we are stuck in an earth-suit. This, however, has been the Life of my relationship; intimate time alone with God.

Before I go on, I want to be clear. I do pray on my knees. I also pray on my back, in the bathroom, while driving a car etc. But I am speaking here of time solely for God; time where nothing else distracts me. Time where I speak little unless in the spirit and I listen intently. This kind of time cannot be penciled in or made to fit. This kind of time is a dedicated, set aside time and place, where you and Holy Spirit spend time alone. As you minister quietly to God and as you make Him the priority in your life; your life will change and you will leave behind that illusion that hurts you daily. This cannot be a "by chance" thing; you need to make this an "on purpose" decision. Turn off the TV, get off the social media platforms, make EVERYTHING else scheduled around your time with Him. Cut out ministry if He leads you to, and make HIM your Life and you will have Life and Life more abundantly. Remember; when you get into your "prayer closet" SHUT THE DOOR! Let nothing distract you. If you have kids, wake up before they do or find a time. Leave the excuses behind. Learn to be still and listen because what God has to say to me is so much more important than what I have to say to Him.

To be able to minister to God, you have to know Him. To say you "know" Him includes His likes, His dislikes, etc. Does He like pecan pie? Have you asked Him? What does He want you to wear? Have you asked Him? You have to spend time with Him to build a relationship. The challenge is that many give up after a few obstacles, and they feel like this "prayer thing" is not for them. That is a lie. Here is the foolproof recipe. Start small. I started with fifteen minutes and could have sworn I was in there a few hours. As fifteen minutes became easier, I progressed to thirty then sixty, etc. If you are reading this and are thinking SIXTY MINUTES! Too much! I hear you, and I recognize those thoughts in the soul-realm. I was there once, then I decided to mature. What are you deciding to do?

This is the one and only *advice* I can give you. Prayer and intimate alone time with Him are key. Learn to listen and recognize **HIS** voice over the other voices of your past and self-will that bounce around in your head, pulling you left and right. Learn to be still in the spirit and at peace. God wants us to be raised up into Christ-likeness. *Ephesians 4:11-16* should be read by all Christians, especially in the Amplified version of the Bible. He wants you to achieve maturity to resemble Christ now, and to walk in His Love. What are you being molded into? Church pew-warmer? Church server? Ministry to man seeker? …Or Christ?

The importance of understanding you are spirit, have a soul, and live in a body, is so important, that I ask you read this book several times and seek His understanding of this. I have total faith you will be set free and be a captive no longer, to your past, or in that false reality that looks to suffocate you. It took me a long time dealing with distractions, both in and outside of the "church", before I could see the little that He allowed me to. I pray you start to see yourself as God does; a spirit being, a temple, and in need to pull aside and have relationship with God as Father. No matter how deep your relationship is, seeing yourself apart from flesh and soul will only bring you closer to Him and expedite your maturity.

My only desire is to see the Christ built up in you, and if we meet before His return, I pray you can see the Christ in me before I speak.

And now for the rest of the story…

Part Three

The end of the story and the beginning of a revolution

As I exited the bathroom, I was hoping I could find an available seat on such a busy night. I was shocked to see the same comfy chair I saw earlier still empty on a night like this. The gentleman with the gray beard was still there. I sat down next to him, and I thought "I will sit here until I have to go to the bathroom again. That way, rather than being stuck in a car, I am only 20 feet from the restroom." I felt very smart.

As I started reading the second comic book, the gentleman leaned over and said "Before you start your reading, do you mind if I ask you a question?"

I said, "Yes sir, go ahead."

He looked at me and said, "Do you consider yourself a black man?"

I looked at him and thought: "This old fool has no idea whom he is speaking to. A Harlemnite from New York, born in the Bronx, raised in Harlem, black history expert, teacher on ethnic differences and races. HA! This old fool just walked into a classroom." I then proceeded to speak. I shared with Him how, why, and "how come" I was a "black man." I threw in Biblical examples of ethnic encounters and made a foolproof case.

He had listened intently and had held my gaze with eyes of steel. Without blinking or looking away he said; "Do you mind if I ask you another question?"

I shook my head no, and he asked me "What color is your watch?"

"Black," I responded.

"What color is your shoe?" he asked.

"Black," I said again.

"What color are your pants?"

I affirmed again, "Black."

Then he asked, "What color is your skin?"

And I said, "Well, brown."

And he asked me, "Is that the same as black?"

I said "No; it is not sir."

"Well then, why would you say you were black? I mean if I was your second grade teacher, and I asked you to show me a black crayon, and you held up a brown one, I may have to consider holding you back a year."

I smiled at this. It actually made sense, why did we say "black?"

Then he asked me "Why are you associating yourself with flesh?"

I answered, "Well, I am flesh."

And so began his real line of questioning. I did not know it, but I was before a very experienced fisher of men, and I was entangled in a net I never saw coming.

He asked me "If you were on the moon, what kind of suit would you need?"

I said; "A space suit."

"Correct," he said. "And if you were underwater what kind of suit would you need?"

I answered, "A scuba or diving suit."

"Correct again," he said. "Now man is a spirit, and when God created man what do you think He needed for man to function fully and interact on earth?"

I slowly said, "An earth-suit?"

And as he smiled I knew my life would never be the same. I realized then that it was Holy Spirit that had worked in me-to get me to stop at the bookstore for this divine encounter. I thought that I was being led by a biological need, but I had been guided by Holy Spirit!

That was half a decade ago, and my walk has never been the same. My relationship is still in need of more of Him, more growth, more intimacy and more revelations of Him in me. Yet I press on to the ONLY thing that matters; relationship in spirit with Truth.

Enjoy my other books, and may He lead you into more of His glory as you seek first his Kingdom and His Way of Living.

Daniel

A Note from the Author

In my other books (soon to be released), listed below, you will be able to read about the paths I have taken and how I got back up from hard falls in Christ:

- Living God
- Loving God
- Listening God
- Single for God
- It's All God

These are not "how-to" books and certainly NOT "do-it-yourself books." On the contrary, these are "How He said it should be done, for and WITH Him", books. I do not feel it is my place to "tell you" how to draw closer to God. I am, however, sharing what the Lord wants from anyone that is born-again and saved. My intention in Him, and His intention through me, is to get you away from reliance on your own understanding, and to trust in Him at all times. These books are a gift of His revelations to me that will assist you to grow in HIM, as you sincerely apply what you read, and earnestly seek HIS presence. I write as I walk these out and see them manifest more of Him in my life.

These books take you from a false identity in soul-realm and dependency on flesh, into your True identity in Christ as a spirit-man. I pray and have an expectancy that they serve as guides, leading you into a deeper revelation of Him in YOU, and of you in HIM. Amen?

Daniel Isaiah Shalach
Bond-servant

ALL I want to be, and All I want to BE, is in Him.

Visit us @ **www.LookingGod.com**
Friend us @ **https://www.facebook.com/LookingGod**

www.ingramcontent.com/pod-product-compliance
Lightning Source LLC
LaVergne TN
LVHW051509070426
835507LV00022B/3006